Lecture Notes in Artificial Intelligence   11422

Subseries of Lecture Notes in Computer Science

More information about this series at http://www.springer.com/series/1244

Donghui Lin · Toru Ishida ·
Franco Zambonelli · Itsuki Noda (Eds.)

Massively Multi-Agent Systems II

International Workshop, MMAS 2018
Stockholm, Sweden, July 14, 2018
Revised Selected Papers

 Springer

Editors
Donghui Lin ⓘ
Kyoto University
Kyoto, Japan

Toru Ishida ⓘ
Kyoto University
Kyoto, Japan

Franco Zambonelli ⓘ
University of Modena and Reggio Emilia
Reggio Emilia, Italy

Itsuki Noda ⓘ
National Institute of Advanced Industrial
Science and Technology (AIST)
Tsukuba, Japan

ISSN 0302-9743   ISSN 1611-3349   (electronic)
Lecture Notes in Artificial Intelligence
ISBN 978-3-030-20936-0   ISBN 978-3-030-20937-7   (eBook)
https://doi.org/10.1007/978-3-030-20937-7

LNCS Sublibrary: SL7 – Artificial Intelligence

This Springer imprint is published by the registered company Springer Nature Switzerland AG
The registered company address is: Gewerbestrasse 11, 6330 Cham, Switzerland

Preface

In 2004, the First International Workshop on Massively Multi-agent Systems (MMAS 2004), was held in Kyoto, Japan. It covered several areas related to massively multi-agent systems in the public space: massively multi-agent technology, teams and organization, ubiquitous computing, and ambient intelligence. At that workshop, the discussion centered on why MMAS should be the focus of attention in the era of ubiquitous computing and networking rather than just multi-agent systems (MAS).

Today, we are witnessing the rapid growth of the Internet of Things (IoT), where millions of physical devices with computing facilities are connected with each other in ad hoc ways, but are required to behave coherently. Massively multi-agent systems can be a major design paradigm or an implementation method for IoT and other large-scale distributed systems.

The 2018 International Workshop on Massively Multi-agent Systems (MMAS 2018) was held on July 14, 2018, in Stockholm, Sweden, and was co-located with the 27th International Joint Conference on Artificial Intelligence and the 23rd European Conference on Artificial Intelligence (IJCAI-ECAI 2018), the 17th International Conference on Autonomous Agents and Multiagent Systems (AAMAS 2018), and the 35th International Conference on Machine Learning (ICML 2018). The aim of MMAS 2018 was to provide a forum for researchers to discuss enabling technologies, new architectures, promising applications, and challenges of massively multi-agent systems in the era of IoT.

The MMAS 2018 workshop featured four invited speakers: Franco Zambonelli from the University of Modena and Reggio Emilia, who explained key enabling technologies and challenges of distributed speaking objects as a case for massively multi-agent systems; Itsuki Noda from the National Institute of Advanced Industrial Science and Technology, Japan, who presented real applications of massively multi-agent systems in social systems like urban traffic control and disaster response; Andrea Omicini from the University of Bologna, who discussed the potential of logic-based approaches for massively multi-agent systems; and Yohei Murakami from Ritsumeikan University, who introduced a new architecture for distributed massively multi-agent systems with example scenarios in the real world. The workshop included seven oral presentations, which were categorized into two parts: multi-agent systems and IoT, architectures for massively multi-agent systems.

This volume consists of ten papers: seven revised papers presented at the workshop and three post-workshop papers. The post-workshop papers focused on applications of massively multi-agent systems, including two invited papers: Feldman and Bucchiarone introduced the transportation as a service (TaaS) as a massively multi-agent system able to cover a diverse technological spectrum ranging from tightly structured hierarchies to open markets; and Murase et al. presented a software framework called CARAVAN, which was developed for comprehensive simulations on massive parallel computers.

We hope this book will encourage researchers in their efforts to develop new massively multi-agent systems and applications, and to explore how massively multi-agent systems can be used for large-scale social design with big data analysis, high-performance computing, and other leading technologies. We are grateful to all the Organizing Committee members, Program Committee members, workshop presenters and participants, post-workshop authors, and those who have supported this workshop.

March 2019
                                                                    Donghui Lin
                                                                    Toru Ishida
                                                                    Franco Zambonelli
                                                                    Itsuki Noda

Organization

Workshop Organizers

Donghui Lin	Kyoto University, Japan
Toru Ishida	Kyoto University, Japan
Franco Zambonelli	University of Modena and Reggio Emilia, Italy
Alexis Drogoul	UMI UMMISCO 209, IRD and UPMC, France
Munindar P. Singh	North Carolina State University, USA
Tomohisa Yamashita	Hokkaido University, Japan
Itsuki Noda	National Institute of Advanced Industrial Science and Technology, Japan

Program Committee

Jake Beal	BBN Technologies, USA
Peter Lewis	Aston University, UK
Andrea Omicini	University of Bologna, Italy
Patrick Taillandier	INRA, Toulouse, France
Hiromitsu Hattori	Ritsumeikan University, Japan
Toshiharu Sugawara	Waseda University, Japan
Yohei Murakami	Ritsumeikan University, Japan
Norman Sadeh	Carnegie Mellon University, USA
Amit K. Chopra	Lancaster University, UK
Donghui Lin	Kyoto University, Japan
Toru Ishida	Kyoto University, Japan
Franco Zambonelli	University of Modena and Reggio Emilia, Italy
Alexis Drogoul	UMI UMMISCO 209, IRD and UPMC, France
Munindar P. Singh	North Carolina State University, USA
Tomohisa Yamashita	Hokkaido University, Japan
Itsuki Noda	National Institute of Advanced Industrial Science and Technology, Japan

Sponsor

Grant-in-Aid for Scientific Research (A) (No. 17H00759), JSPS
Grant-in-Aid for Scientific Research (B) (No. 18H03341), JSPS

Contents

Multi-agent Systems and Internet of Things

Distributed Speaking Objects: A Case for Massive Multiagent Systems

Marco Lippi$^{(\boxtimes)}$ iD, Marco Mamei iD, Stefano Mariani iD,
and Franco Zambonelli iD

Dipartimento di Scienze e Metodi dell'Ingegneria,
Università di Modena e Reggio Emilia, Reggio Emilia, Italy
{marco.lippi,marco.mamei,stefano.mariani,franco.zambonelli}@unimore.it

Abstract. Smart sensors and actuators, embedding learning and reasoning features and associated to everyday objects and locations, will
soon densely populate our everyday environments. Being capable of
understanding, reasoning, and reporting about what is happening (for
sensors) and about what they can make possibly happen (for actuators), these "speaking objects" will thus be assimilable to autonomous
situated agents. Accordingly, populations of speaking objects will define
dense and massive multiagent systems, devoted to monitor and control
our environments, let them be homes, industries or, in the large-scale,
whole cities. In this context, the necessary coordination among speaking objects will be likely to become associated with the capability of
argumenting about situations and about the current state of the affairs,
triggering and directing proper distributed conversations, and eventually
collectively reach future desirable state of the affairs. In this article, we
detail the speaking objects vision, overview the key enabling technologies, and analyze the key challenges for engineering large-scale collectives
of speaking objects and their conversations.

Keywords: Massive multiagent systems · Internet of Things ·
Argumentation

1 Introduction

The *Internet of Things* (IoT) is enabled by the possibility of enriching physical
objects and places with wirelessly accessible sensing, computing, and actuating
capabilities [3], such that everything in our physical and social worlds will become
a node in a large-scale situated network, supporting coordinated actions to sense
and control the world itself and to facilitate interactions with it [5].

As of today, most of the approaches to engineer IoT systems still consider
IoT devices as simple providers of services, either sensing services producing
raw data or actuating services executing specific *commands* [3]. From the architectural viewpoint, most approaches adopt a *centralized*, often cloud-based perspective: raw sensor data is collected at some control point, there analyzed to

© Springer Nature Switzerland AG 2019
D. Lin et al. (Eds.): MMAS 2018, LNAI 11422, pp. 3–20, 2019.
https://doi.org/10.1007/978-3-030-20937-7_1

infer situations and events in the concerns of interest, and commands for the actuators are generated to have them produce some effect on the smart objects in the environment in which they situate. However, some recent technological evolutions [1, 9, 34] let us point to a novel scenario:

- IoT devices can and are going to become much smarter [9]. On the one hand, rather than simply producing streams of data, smart sensors can integrate Artificial Intelligence (AI) tools, thus becoming capable of *understanding* and reporting – via factual assertions and arguments – about what is happening around. On the other hand, smart actuators will become increasingly autonomous and *goal-oriented*, and able to decide how to act towards the achievement of specific goals [1]. In other words, such smart objects are becoming de facto software agents or, as we like to call them, "speaking objects" [24].
- Multitudes of speaking objects will form the nodes of massive distributed multiagent systems that can be exploited to monitor and control activities in real-time in our everyday environment. Although centralized cloud-based approaches are here to stay for the sake of global data analysis and long-term planning, speaking objects will have to interact and coordinate with each other in a distributed way, to ensure prompt response to local situations [34].

Clearly, the very nature of speaking objects will dramatically change the approaches to implementing and coordinating the activities of distributed processes. In fact, coordination is likely to become associated with the capability of *argumenting* about situations and about the current "state of the affairs" [9], by reaching a consensus on what is happening around and what is needed, and by triggering and directing proper decentralised semantic *conversations* to decide how to collectively act in order to reach future desirable state of the affairs.

In this context, the paper provides the following contributions:

- An analysis of the key concepts behind speaking objects, showing how they are going to change the very nature of decentralized coordination and are going to challenge traditional approaches to distributed computing and calling for novel *conversational* approaches.
- An overview of the key technologies and approaches that, in such a novel scenario, will have to be involved in the engineering of systems and services, and will have to become core expertise for distributed systems engineering. Among the others, these include knowledge representation and *commonsense* reasoning, *machine learning*, *goal-oriented* programming, *argumentation* models and technologies, and *human-computer* interfaces.
- The identification of some research challenges that will have to be faced to pave the way towards a novel and effective approach for the engineering of these new classes of distributed systems. These include challenges at the level of software engineering models, middleware technologies, user involvement, control and understandability, security.

To ground the discussion with an exemplary case study, we will consider the case of a large-scale deployment where a *smart hospital* is instrumented to support health monitoring and assisted living [16]. We assume the hospital to be densely enriched with connected sensors and actuators, at the level of basic infrastructures (e.g., lightening, heating), all its rooms (with ambient cameras, controllable doors and windows), appliances (e.g., furniture, clocks, TV, fridge, etc.), and medical devices (e.g., spirometers, heartbeat monitoring devices, Fitbits, etc.). This infrastructure, possibly including wearable bio and activity sensors, can be used to monitor the living and health conditions of patients, and to dynamically control the overall configuration of the hospital to fit peculiar needs and contingencies.

2   Speaking Objects as Cognitive Goal-Oriented Agents

Currently, in the IoT arena (and in related typical application scenarios, from smart homes to smart cities and transportation) the concept of *smart object* is mostly associated to the possibility of attaching ICT devices to physical objects and places, thus turning them into: *(i) sensors*, capable of sensing a large amount of properties related to our physical/social worlds, and producing big streams of data to be collected at some centralized (or semi-centralized as in edge/fog computing approaches [39]) point for later analysis; *(ii)* remotely controllable *actuators*, capable of enacting specific configurations or actions in the surrounding environment, by receiving appropriate commands.

Progress across many different areas, though, indicates that smart objects are improving fast beyond such mere sensing and actuating capabilities, to become capable of cognitive goal-oriented behavior. That is, to become de facto autonomous agents.

2.1   Data Collection vs. Cognitive Sensing

Advancements in machine learning techniques, and in the increase of computational power that can be embedded in everyday sensors and objects, is making it possible for smart objects to analyze *locally* the stream of sensed data in order to extract relevant features from it. A simple example, in our case study scenario, is a set of wearable devices monitoring physiological parameters and physical activities of a patient, capable of associating the sensed patterns of movement to situations like "unusual heart rate", "walking", "running" (see Fig. 1), or a control camera that detects the presence of specific objects in the recorded scene, such as "stretcher in corridor X". To some extent, such objects are already becoming "speaking", by evolving from producers of raw data streams (a capability that they nevertheless preserve) to producers of high-level concepts.

However, we can soon expect that such capabilities will evolve in order to recognize more complex situations, making objects capable of *causally* connecting individual patterns into composite situations, that is, making assertions about what is happening around them. For instance, a set of wearables may construct the assertion that "Heart rate increased due to a training session" from the sensing of two distinct patterns. Or a camera may perform scene understanding, by

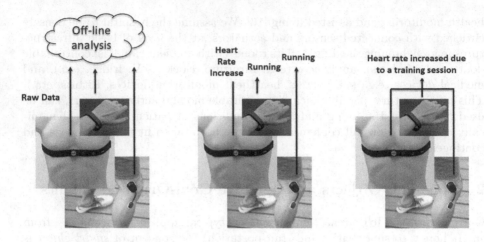

Fig. 1. From simple sensors to speaking objects. In a smart hospital scenario a number of wearable devices can interact – speak – to gather a complete description of a situation.

relating the individual objects it recognizes, e.g., "patient Marco has left the stretcher in corridor X". Such complex *situation recognition* is a hot topic for research in computer vision and in pervasive computing in general [38].

Further capabilities of asserting about complex situations arise from *sensor fusion* techniques, where the outputs of multiple sensors – each with a specific perspective on the surrounding world – are combined together to form a more comprehensive understanding. For example, fusing information from a camera and a temperature sensor in a smart room can eventually enable to assert that "the temperature is dropping down because the window is open".

Last but not least, the possibility for humans to enter the picture and act themselves as speaking objects (e.g., by posting information via their mobile phones), brings further possibilities of complex event recognition to the scenario.

In any case, our concept of *speaking objects* should not be interpreted solely as the capability of interacting via natural language (which nevertheless is an important feature in the overall framework, as we will discuss in the following) but more generally as the capability of expressing and understanding *assertions* about situations, regardless of the media and language which they are delivered with.

2.2   Actuating Commands vs. Achieving Goals

Concerning actuators, our perspective is that smart actuating objects (capable of performing some action in the environment) will become capable of "hearing" what are the goals or situations to be achieved, and achieve them *autonomously*.

Again, we emphasize here that it is not a matter of having smart tools (such as Amazon Echo or Google Home) capable of interpreting vocal commands to activate some home appliances. In fact, whether triggered by vocal commands or by traditional service invocations, current appliances are simply interpreting *commands* and executing them. We are rather talking of moving from a command-based mode of operation to a *goal-based* one. Instead of telling actuators what to do, a goal-based approach relies on expressing a desirable *state of the affairs* to be achieved with respect to some environmental configuration, and let them autonomously evaluate what actions to make in order to reach it.

For instance, in the hospital scenario, a patient can simply express some desire (e.g., "I need to sleep") and have the light system start operating in autonomy, adjusting lightning accordingly. Or, a smart desk lamp that autonomously moves and tunes intensity to ensure optimal illumination in spite of changing environmental conditions [1].

Smart actuator objects, to achieve their goals, must acquire information about the current state of the affairs, which requires gathering information from smart sensors. Also, they must sometimes interact with each other and with non-smart objects (e.g., non goal-oriented actuators). For instance, in order to achieve specific temperature and humidity comfort levels, the A/C system might be in need to cooperate with the heating system and should be allowed to operate the opening/closing of the windows (assuming such windows as non goal-oriented).

The requirement of *interaction* brings us to the next section.

3 Distributed Coordination as a Conversation

In an environment populated by smart speaking objects (e.g., sensors) and by a variety of smart hearing objects (e.g., actuators), the issue of *coordinating* their distributed activities arises. In fact (see Fig. 2):

- Speaking objects sense and have to produce an understanding of the situations around, for which they may be in need to exchange information (to complete information or to disambiguate it).
- Speaking objects have to talk with hearing objects to inform them about what is happening (the current state of the affairs and the *reasons* causing them), which is necessary for hearing objects to plan actions.
- Hearing objects may have to talk to each other to agree on common courses of actions, whenever a desired state of the affairs (either embedded in their code or dynamically expressed at run-time) requires the cooperation of multiple actuators, or may be achieved in multiple ways by different actuators, or multiple conflicting views of the desired state of the affairs exist.
- All of which to form a *closed loop* [19], in which any action by the actuators produces some changes in the environment that have to be immediately sensed to provide feedback for the actuator themselves. Given such dynamics, and the possibility of expressing new desires in real-time, centralized (e.g., in the cloud) approaches become unsuitable, whereas *decentralized* coordination between the different objects (and possibly the concerned human actors) becomes mandatory, possibly with the support of some local hub [39].

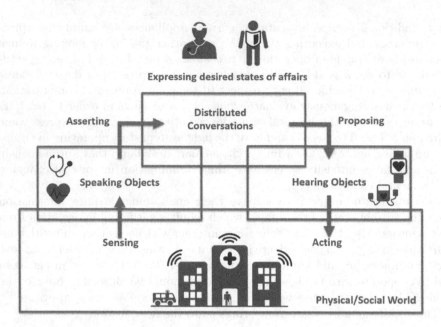

Fig. 2. Coordination among smart speaking objects and smart hearing actuators has to be realized as a sort of distributed multi-agent conversation. In the smart hospital scenario a massive amount of devices and systems might need to coordinate to obtain a coherent view of the situation.

In the following we show that, in the envisioned scenario, coordination between speaking and hearing objects naturally assumes the form of a distributed multi-party *conversation*, or *dialogue* [2], among autonomous agents.

3.1   From Coordination to Conversations

A *conversation* is a *session of interaction* between an ensemble of distributed agents, with the aim of letting them reach an agreement about their beliefs and/or plans of actions [36]. In the speaking object scenario, conversations take place by having speaking and hearing objects exchange *assertions* about the current or desirable state of the affairs, respectively. Such assertions can be contradicted or strengthened by others engaging in the conversation with the goal of reaching an agreement about the state of the world (for speaking objects) or about a joint plan aimed at achieving a given state of affairs (for hearing objects).

Conversational approaches to distributed coordination are radically different from traditional approaches, which tend to enforce strict rules on the behavior of components, and assume the presence of specific *coordination laws* to respect, in terms of how components interact and how components should behave during interaction. They mostly leave no room for goal-oriented behaviors and for *adapting* the dynamics of a distributed coordination protocol to the actual outcomes of the conversation itself and to the arguments raised by components during the coordination process.

In some sense, conversation-based coordination shifts attention to the *meta-level* of coordination, by providing rules to negotiate interaction protocols rather than the protocols themselves. *Flexibility* greatly benefits from this perspective, because not only the actual interactions among participant components arise at run-time according to a given interaction protocol, but the protocol itself *emerges* from the bottom up. Furthermore, traditional coordination approaches are mostly *memoryless*, as they rarely track the history of interactions for purposes beyond performance tuning, computation of trust, or adaptation of policies. The envisioned conversations, instead, naturally account for interaction history through the notion of *commitment*, aiming to track promises, claims, and arguments, for the sake of correctness of the whole coordination process.

Even in the IoT arena, most approaches for orchestrating the activities of the different components rely, as of today, on a set of *rules*, and on middleware engines that check and enact them [32]. Such rules dictate how the components should be activated (and their services executed), depending both on the situations that are happening, and on those that – in reaction – should be achieved. However, in a scenario of speaking and hearing (goal-oriented) objects, such an approach falls short, due to the impossibility of foreseeing and defining all possible events and state of the affairs, and all the possible ways in which components can be activated. It is in fact unfeasible to design all the possible composition rules that orchestrate the behaviors of the components. Thus, while the possibility of defining rules and constraints for the "do" and the "don't" of the systems (e.g., *safety* and *liveness* properties that should be always guaranteed [40]) should remain, the actual way the components act and interact should be identified at run-time by the components themselves, still in respect of global system goals and constraints.

The issue of reaching a consensus in an ensemble of interacting autonomous components via distributed negotiations has been deeply investigated in the area of *agent-oriented* computing [17]. However, negotiation mechanisms are blind with respect to the strategy adopted by the agents participating in the negotiation. This does not help in reaching globally satisfactory solutions, which could be achieved instead by letting agents conversate and motivate their choices, as proposed in *argumentation-based* multi-agent negotiation [30], a research area that has very strong relations with our vision (see Sect. 4.4).

3.2 Types of Conversations

Let us now classify the different types of conversation that one can expect to take place in the speaking objects scenario.

Among Speaking Objects. Speaking objects are likely to interact with each other in order to build and report a complete and coherent understanding of their surroundings. However, it may be the case that the identification of a specific situation requires *(i)* more information than initially thought, or *(ii)* solving some conflicting perceptions.

The former case triggers what are called *information seeking* and *inquiry dialogues* [36]. These are aimed at integrating the originally incomplete information with either new information or more arguments in support of the existing one. For example, in the smart hospital scenario, a set of speaking cameras need to ask each other who they are detecting to collectively build a global map of patients' locations in real-time.

In the latter case, different (sets of) speaking objects may reach different conclusions about what is happening, which triggers *negotiation* and *persuasion dialogues* to let them all agree on a common perspective. To this end, speaking objects may exchange arguments explaining the reasons why they ended up identifying a specific situation to persuade others, or they may decide to involve additional sensors in the conversation. In the smart hospital scenario, the variety of speaking objects may not necessarily acquire the same perspective on what is sensed. A camera in the rehabilitation room of the hospital may recognize that a man is "running on the treadmill", the treadmill itself may state that the user is "standing", whereas the wristband may recognize that he is "jumping". To solve the conflict, they may start comparing with each other the reasons behind their respective understandings of the situation. This can enable discovering that, since the treadmill is off (and this is why it stated that the user was "standing"), the only reasonable explanation is that "the user is jumping on the treadmill".

We emphasize that, although a variety of sensor fusion techniques exist to support situation identification [22], these typically act downstream the sensor level, as they simply receive data from sensors and try to apply well-defined rules to both integrate distinct data streams and solve possible conflicts. Basically, they are mostly *black-boxes* from an observer standpoint. Moreover, they do not usually consider giving sensors the possibility of taking action themselves. Yet, in our view speaking sensor objects become sort of *grey-boxes*: they can be requested to *justify* their perceptions and *explain* their course of action, and are expected to provide insights into the reasoning that guides their behavior. The same holds for hearing actuator objects, as described in the following.

Between Speaking and Hearing Objects. While planning for a specific course of action aimed at achieving a given state of the affairs, hearing objects may recognize that they need more information and/or more convincing arguments than initially provided in order to make an informed decision.

This kind of conversation is a mixture of *information seeking, inquiry*, and *deliberation* dialogues [36], which should be suitably composed so as to enable informed decision making: in this way, hearing actuators are able to plan and justify their course of actions based on the amount and quality of information required by the scenario at hand. Notice that this kind of closed *feedback loop* between sensing and acting is very expensive with state of the art cloud-based approach to IoT.

Among Hearing Objects. In the majority of real world applications, such as in the assisted living scenario already described, it is quite unusual that actuators are able to *individually* change their environment (namely, act) so as to achieve the optimal state of affairs. Rather, it is usually through collaboration and joint planning efforts that the most effective and efficient strategy to achieve a given goal can be designed and pursued. Accordingly, it is often the case that hearing objects engage in *deliberation* dialogues meant to achieve a *shared plan* by exchanging arguments about feasibility of actions, their expected utility, likelihood of positive/negative outcomes, and the like. Then, it is similarly unrealistic to assume that the landscape of all the possible actions by all the participant actuators is *conflict-free* [43]. Thus, *negotiation* and *persuasion* dialogues are required as a means to argue toward conflicts resolution.

As an example, consider an A/C system in a room of the hospital willing to turn itself on after hearing the thermostat assert "it's hot". In case a few hearing windows are also installed, both the A/C and the windows may decide to act, without actually generating any conflict: either turning on the A/C or opening the windows (or doing both) leads to the goal anyway. Nevertheless, doing both is sub-optimal from the standpoint of efficiency, thus joint deliberation to *collectively* choose an individual course of action or a shared plan – in this case, who acts and who doesn't – is likely welcome. Accordingly, the window may convince the A/C not to act by argumenting "there is a fresh breeze outside, I can save power consumption while still chilling the room". Now consider the same scenario during the summer: if both actuators act there is a conflict, because the air coming from the outside would likely be hot, actually neglecting the air conditioning effect—or, at the very least, hindering the A/C system course of actions and leading to sub-optimal efficiency and effectiveness. Yet again, thus, joint deliberation for shared planning is required.

4   Enabling Technologies

Let us now present the main technologies and approaches which enable our vision. Although these have been widely investigated in the context of agents and multiagent systems, they are not (yet) properly accounted for by research in the IoT area.

4.1   Cognitive Reasoning

First of all, given their conversational nature, speaking and hearing objects need to implement some form of cognitive reasoning, and especially of *knowledge representation* and *commonsense reasoning*. By continuously interacting among them and with humans through dialogue, they will have to share a common representation of the world.

A clear need is that of exploiting knowledge bases and large-scale ontologies to model and represent the concepts and their relations, which the agents continuously deal with. This issue represents a significant challenge in agent coordination [10] and it remains under-explored in the IoT domain [14]. Although the general problem is far from being solved, yet some recent works have proposed architectures that address the aforementioned issues. For example, in [11] a framework is proposed, that builds lower- and higher-level abstractions, starting from raw data. A recent survey [29] presents several approaches to context-aware computing in the IoT domain, with a specific emphasis on their capability to embed background knowledge and context-awareness. Such thorough analysis shows how *rule-based* mechanisms are still largely employed to perform symbolic reasoning, thanks to the hand-crafted knowledge bases designed by experts. An analysis of the scalability of this kind of technologies towards massive systems has been recently presented [25], together with an experimental evaluation of the most promising semantic reasoning approaches in the IoT arena.

Commonsense reasoning also has to be integrated into the scenario of speaking and hearing objects. This keyword describes a research area where the aim is to make computers capable of performing those basic inference processes that we, as humans, continuously perform without even thinking [8]. This skill is crucial in our everyday life, and allows us to take decisions and solve problems. Smart devices that will be more and more integrated in our life, such as speaking and hearing objects, will necessarily embed this ability in order to autonomously and proactively operate. Currently, existing approaches are limited to restricted domains and, therefore, to restricted reasoning capabilities (typically, taxonomic reasoning) [8]. We argue that large-scale scenarios will provide novel data collections upon which it will be possible to test new techniques, for example coming from machine learning.

4.2 Machine Learning

Massively distributed sensors in the IoT arena clearly produce huge data streams, that need manipulation, aggregation, and sometimes also more sophisticated, intelligent elaboration. These steps are nowadays often performed directly on-board, within smart sensors, that can embed tools such as deep networks [20]. Turning the processed information into high-level knowledge is, however, still an open issue [29].

Another peculiar trait of speaking and hearing objects is the capability of learning behaviors, strategies, and policies from historical data and situations, with the aim of continuously adapting to the environment. This would represent a major advantage with respect to approaches based on sets of pre-defined, hand-crafted rules, that are clearly hard to update in case of abrupt system changes. Similarly, pattern mining methodologies could be exploited to perform association rule mining and user profiling [35]. Here, we believe that Statistical Relational Learning [13] and Neural-Symbolic learning [12] could offer a valuable research direction to pursue, as they propose to combine logic-based approaches with statistical learning, probabilistic models, and neural approaches (including deep learning), with the goal of both handling uncertainty in data, and exploiting background knowledge. The idea is that grey-box models, capable of exploiting both the computational power of systems such as deep networks, and the interpretability of logic and argumentation, will offer tools to support medium and long-term self-adaptation of pervasive computing systems. In this way, speaking objects will move a step towards *explainable artificial intelligence*, which is considered one of the major challenges for the near future.

4.3   Goal-Oriented Computing

Making actuators become goal-oriented requires to ascribe them a few crucial capabilities: *(i)* recognize expression of a goal, as a state of affairs to be achieved; *(ii)* *deliberate* whether they may play a role in pursuing that goal, and how; *(iii)* *reason* about feasibility, likelihood of success, and outcomes of the actions needed to get there [37]; *(iv)* *plan* the course of actions to undertake, considering cost, expected utility, etc. [27]. All of this in *autonomy*, that is, with the opportunity to reject goals if they are not of interest, abandon them if they are no longer feasible, offer help to others if such an opportunity arises, and ask help to others if no other means to achieve the goal is currently available.

It is worth noting that goal-oriented behaviour may be ascribed to speaking objects as well. In the current IoT vision, sensors are simply *hard-coded* to monitor a given property of a given environment, to generate data and events accordingly. In the speaking objects vision, instead, sensors may bind monitoring activities to an *explicit* and *dynamic* goal, either expressed by another component or by a human user.

It is then necessary to embed at the very foundation of the speaking objects vision all the concepts, abstractions, and models commonly found in the *agent-oriented* literature, such as the notion of cognitive agents [31], techniques for means-ends reasoning [37] and planning [27], the many issues of coordination in multi-agent systems [28]. Many languages and infrastructures have proven to be mature enough for relevant scenarios in the agent-based community: for a survey, the interested reader is referred to [4]. Yet, their viability and effectiveness in a highly dynamic, heterogeneous, resource-constrained, and scale-demanding domain such as IoT, still remains to be fully assessed.

4.4   Argumentation-Based Coordination

Argumentation is required as a necessary feature of sensor and actuator devices to regard them as speaking and hearing objects. Argumentation may in fact well support: *(i)* *decentralised coordination*, by leveraging negotiation opportunities; *(ii)* *situated reasoning*, by enabling belief revision in face of uncertainty; *(iii)* *joint deliberation*, by allowing negotiation over desires and plans besides beliefs; *(iv)* *"humans-in-the-loop"*, by making explanations and justifications of decision making available in natural language. For a more thorough analysis of these aspects, the reader may refer to [23].

Despite the long history of research in argumentation, only recently practical applications to real-world scenarios have started receiving attention (e.g., see [18]). Furthermore, for argumentation to work there must be either an agreement among participants about the *admissible moves* and their significance, or an *external judge* enacting some form of control over the argumentation process. Neither of the two is straightforward to have in the speaking objects vision:

reaching agreement is difficult *per se*, besides being unlikely easily scalable; and having an external authority may be an unacceptable centralisation point. A way out can be found by carefully investigating *hybrid* approaches where, for instance, a multitude of external authorities share the load of arbitrating argumentations among a limited number of participants, possibly exploiting some notion of physical or logical proximity to enforce shared argumentation rules. Another solution could be to have participants agree only temporarily, for the duration of a given "conversation session" on a common set of argumentation rules, which may then change for future conversations depending on, e.g., timing constraints or the type of dialogue.

5   Integration Recipe: Open Challenges for Realizing the Vision

Although we identified some technologies that will most likely become key ingredients in the speaking objects vision, actually realizing the vision implies having the appropriate modelling tools and middleware infrastructures to coherently integrate them, and to ensure they will be employed to produce practical, usable, and dependable systems.

5.1   Massive Scale and Heterogeneity

The key challenge in developing and controlling systems of distributed speaking objects is their massive overall scale. It is foreseen that in the near future billions of IoT devices will populate our cities, including thousands of our buildings and homes. Such myriads of devices will be in need to be coordinated at different scales, from the global ones (e.g., for achieving policies at urban level) to the local ones (i.e., for realizing functionalities and achieving policies at building or home level).

The computational power of these smart devices is growing faster and faster, allowing to embed very advanced technologies in relatively cheap hardware. This will be a key factor for a massive distribution of intelligent, autonomus agents. In fact, this enables efficient *separation of concerns*, that is distributing functionalities and responsibilities, among the different scales of the system, so as to better tackle the most pressing issues at the right level of abstraction: for instance, critical functionalities requiring rapid decision making and adaptation for quickly solving local contingencies can be attributed to the smaller scale of the multi-scale system at hand (such as an hospital), up to the individual device, whereas medium and long term planning and scheduling of strategic actions can be charged upon the higher scales of the system (i.e., a department-wide in-house server scheduling appointments, or a hospital-wide cloud-based platform planning resource exploitation).

Accordingly, on the one hand it will be needed to design and deploy coordination schemes that can support coordination among a very large number of distributed components, to realize global policies. However, these can hardly rely on conversations and argumentation-based approaches, whose scalability remains an open issue. Rather, they should get inspiration from social and nature-inspired coordination models [42]. On the other hand, the above forms of large-scale coordination should co-exist with more local, argumentation-based, forms of coordination to achieve local goals. How the two forms of coordination could co-exist is definitely an open and fascinating research challenge.

In the case of the hospital deployment already mentioned, for instance, the system may be conceptually – and technically, actually, as explained in the following – split in a few layers, corresponding to the different scales at which it is conveniently modelled and designed; let us assume three as depicted in Fig. 3:

- the smaller scale is mostly concerned with local-only, critical, highly dynamic situations recognition and decision making (i.e. a single room where a patient may unexpectedly need the emergency unit)
- the medium scale is possibly the most difficult to define, since it is essentially meant to transition from the local perspective of the smaller one to the global-perspective of the larger one. Here, the most critical task is that of defining how information coming from the lower layer (the smaller scale) can be aggregated and presented to the upper layer (the larger scale), and how decision making executed on the higher layer should be translated in actionable commands for the lower one. For instance, coordination amongst doctors and nurses in the same department based on scheduled appointments and emergency events is likely to happen here
- the larger scale deals with global planning and monitoring, where collection of relevant aggregated information and synthesis of consequential activities happen on a medium to long-term horizon, and responsiveness is usually far less important than accuracy and completeness (of both information collection and decision making). This scale may range from an individual hospital building up to the whole hospital organisation as displaced in different geographical areas—but belonging to the same administration.

5.2   Middleware

Under a more pragmatic perspective, a crucial technical question is to understand the role of middleware in supporting the new means of coordinating distributed components, represented by conversations. In fact, although conversation essentially amounts to message-passing interaction, a mere message-oriented middleware (MOM) would fail addressing its peculiarities [6]. Conversations imply a shared knowledge among interacting components, which cooperatively build upon it a common interpretation of the world based on *logically sound* and related arguments, and cooperatively conceive and commit to a joint plan of actions. MOM is also weak in supporting interaction in a dynamic (i.e. open and mobile) world, where the identities and locations of components are not known in advance, as in the case of speaking objects (and of IoT in general).

Accordingly, the middleware should lean towards a different coordination model, capable of going beyond the rather primitive functionality of MOMs in terms of direct interactions between components. Rather, it should support conversations at an higher level of abstraction, i.e. via an open and shared conversation space enabling conversation among components that do not necessarily have to know each other in advance: for instance, a tuple space. However, unlike traditional tuple space models, which contain unrelated pieces of data, the need to access data and metadata about conversations implies connecting information into sorts of *knowledge networks*, detailing how conversations evolved and how they are related. Although some proposals in that direction exist [26], the best way to realize such shared conversation space is still subject of active research. As it is yet to be evaluated how corpora of commonsense knowledge could be integrated within the overall architecture to support conversations.

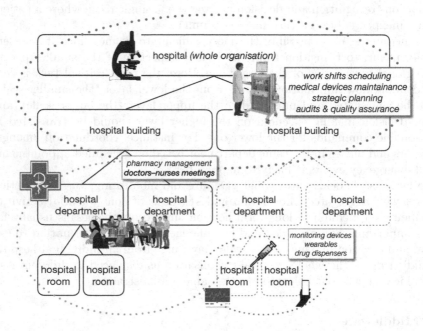

Fig. 3. Different scales of information collection, decision making, and coordination as seen in a large-scale Speaking Objects deployment. Smaller scales are associated with critical, highly dynamic situations, in which argumentation-based coordination may be employed to guarantee soundness and accountability of solutions, whereas larger scales with longer planning and monitoring, and slower but steady adaptation given by self-organising coordination may come handy to manage complexities.

5.3   Humans-in-the-Loop

The speaking objects vision cannot overlook *humans-in-the-loop* as a vital computational component of the scenario. In fact, besides participating as actors that impose their desired states of the affairs to the system (see Fig. 2), humans can become actual components of the system itself: they can participate by providing sensing capabilities (thus acting as speaking objects), actuating capa-bilities (as hearing objects), and can consequently be involved in conversations. This convergence between human and software entities is witnessed by many modern *socio-technical systems*, and it demands researchers and practitioners to conceive, design, and develop systems seamlessly interacting with other software systems and with human agents as well.

It is worth noting that when human users enter the picture, the need for argumentation-based conversations is even more evident: the ability of smart objects to justify their stances, in fact, becomes crucial to convince users to effectively participate in the conversational process. Clearly, this may require accounting for socio-cognitive models of action and interaction as they can be observed among human agents, to be suitably transferred to the synthetic domain of conversating speaking objects.

In this perspective, more natural interfaces, such as voice commands or ges-tures, and techniques coming from natural language processing, speech recogni-tion, and computer vision will become essential components of smart objects, as they already are in our smartphones. In this way, less effort will be required to program devices, and users will experience a more direct and *transparent* interac-tion with technology [21]. While the current state of the art is about interacting with a single device or hub (e.g., Amazon' Echo and Google Home), in the near future we envision interacting with *many* at the same time. For example, a voice command will be heard by multiple devices, and each will have to interpret it, as well as to understand its role in the overall fulfillment.

Besides the need for effective means of human-machine interaction, as already discussed in Sect. 4, integrating humans in the loop also challenges the whole software engineering process, the modeling and design of human behaviours and of conversations involving humans, and the functionalities that the middleware should provide to enable integration.

5.4   Harnessing Algocracy

Nowadays, the world in which we are living is becoming more and more dom-inated by algorithms, that by now are daily exploited in a variety of decision-making processes. This novel scenario is typically referred to as an *algocracy* [7]. In such a framework, it is often the case that we act as passive subjects in situations that have been automatically planned and arranged for us by algo-rithms. This could become a crucial issue in the forthcoming years, when these systems will become a reality also on a large scale, for example in the context of smart cities, where the safety and well-being of citizens will largely depend on technology [41].

The scenario of speaking objects moves a step towards an open and *inter-pretable* network of smart devices, with which humans can naturally interact and converse, eventually understanding the choices and decisions of these agents, through argumentation and dialogue. These innovative elements provide a means through which it could be possible to control algocracy, by creating "grey-boxes" whose behavior will be intelligible by an external observer that needs to inspect their way of acting.

5.5 Security

Distributed scenarios for IoT have been extensively studied in terms of security. Many challenges arise in a massive-scale scenario, including authentication, privacy preservation, data integrity, fault tolerance, trust, and governance [33]. The inherent nature of speaking and hearing objects is grounded on conversation. On the one hand, this makes the framework vulnerable to possible system intrusions and attacks, but at the same time it can represent a major advantage against malicious behavior, thanks to interpretable explanations given by speaking objects via argumentation. The research in the field of argumentation-based risk assessment [15] could be turned into automated argumentation-based security. At the same time, the correctness, validity, and strength of the posed arguments could be exploited to assess the reputation of speaking objects, and thus to enforce the concept of trust in the IoT setting.

6 Conclusions

The emergence of speaking objects will dramatically change the approaches to implementing and coordinating the activities of distributed IoT processes and services, calling for bringing in the lessons of massive multiagent systems. Within this new scenario, scalability will soon become a urgent need, which will require the integration of a number of technologies from different research areas. On the one hand, speaking objects will have to implement coordination through learning, reasoning, and especially argumentation, in order to show a behavior easily interpretable also for humans. On the other hand, such a large-scale scenario represents an ideal testbed for novel technologies in the field of distributed and pervasive computing, which will face challenges in the area of software engineering, security, and human-computer interaction.

Acknowledgments. Work supported by the CONNECARE (Personalised Connected Care for Complex Chronic Patients) project (EU H2020-RIA, Contract No. 689802).

References

1. Agrawal, H., Leigh, S.-W., Maes, P.: L'evolved: autonomous and ubiquitous utilities as smart agents. In: ACM International Joint Conference on Pervasive and Ubiquitous Computing, pp. 487–491. ACM, New York (2015)
2. Amgoud, L., Parsons, S.: Agent dialogues with conflicting preferences. In: Meyer, J.-J.C., Tambe, M. (eds.) ATAL 2001. LNCS (LNAI), vol. 2333, pp. 190–205. Springer, Heidelberg (2002). https://doi.org/10.1007/3-540-45448-9_14
3. Atzori, L., Iera, A., Morabito, G.: The internet of things: a survey. Comput. Netw. **54**(15), 2787–2805 (2010)

4. Bordini, R., et al.: A survey of programming languages and platforms for multi-agent systems. Informatica (Ljubljana) **30**(1), 33–44 (2006). Cited by 152

5. Conti, M., et al.: Looking ahead in pervasive computing: challenges and opportunities in the era of cyber-physical convergence. Pervasive Mob. Comput. **8**(1), 2–21 (2012)

6. Curry, E.: Message-oriented middleware. In: Middleware for Communications, pp. 1–28 (2004)

7. Danaher, J.: The threat of algocracy: reality, resistance and accommodation. Philos. Technol. **29**(3), 245–268 (2016)

8. Davis, E., Marcus, G.: Commonsense reasoning and commonsense knowledge in artificial intelligence. Commun. ACM **58**(9), 92–103 (2015)

9. Endler, M., Briot, J.-P., Silva e Silva, F., De Almeida, V.P., Haeusler, E.H.: An approach for real-time stream reasoning for the internet of things. In: Proceedings of the 11th IEEE International Conference on Semantic Computing (ICSC 2017), pp. 348–353. IEEE, San Diego, January 2017

10. Freitas, A., Bordini, R.H., Meneguzzi, F., Vieira, R.: Towards integrating ontologies in multi-agent programming platforms. In: 2015 IEEE/WIC/ACM International Conference on Web Intelligence and Intelligent Agent Technology (WI-IAT), vol. 3, pp. 225–226. IEEE (2015)

11. Ganz, F., Puschmann, D., Barnaghi, P., Carrez, F.: A practical evaluation of information processing and abstraction techniques for the internet of things. IEEE Internet Things J. **2**(4), 340–354 (2015)

12. Garcez, A.S.D., Broda, K.B., Gabbay, D.M.: Neural-Symbolic Learning Systems: Foundations and Applications. Springer Science & Business Media, London (2012)

13. Getoor, L., Taskar, B.: Introduction to Statistical Relational Learning (Adaptive Computation and Machine Learning). The MIT Press, Cambridge (2007)

14. Gyrard, A., Serrano, M., Atemezing, G.A.: Semantic web methodologies, best practices and ontology engineering applied to internet of things. In: 2015 IEEE 2nd World Forum on Internet of Things (WF-IoT), pp. 412–417. IEEE (2015)

15. Ingolfo, S., Siena, A., Mylopoulos, J., Susi, A., Perini, A.: Arguing regulatory compliance of software requirements. Data Knowl. Eng. **87**, 279–296 (2013)

16. Islam, S.R., Kwak, D., Kabir, M.H., Hossain, M., Kwak, K.-S.: The internet of things for health care: a comprehensive survey. IEEE Access **3**, 678–708 (2015)

17. Jennings, N.R., Faratin, P., Lomuscio, A.R., Parsons, S., Wooldridge, M.J., Sierra, C.: Automated negotiation: prospects, methods and challenges. Group Decis. Negot. **10**(2), 199–215 (2001)

18. Jung, H., Tambe, M., Kulkarni, S.: Argumentation as distributed constraint satisfaction: applications and results. In: Proceedings of the Fifth International Conference on Autonomous Agents, AGENTS 2001, pp. 324–331. ACM, New York (2001)

19. Kephart, J.O., Chess, D.M.: The vision of autonomic computing. IEEE Comput. **36**(1), 41–50 (2003)

20. Kortuem, G., Kawsar, F., Sundramoorthy, V., Fitton, D.: Smart objects as building blocks for the internet of things. IEEE Internet Comput. **14**(1), 44–51 (2010)

21. Kranz, M., Holleis, P., Schmidt, A.: Embedded interaction: interacting with the internet of things. IEEE Internet Comput. **14**(2), 46–53 (2010)

22. Liggins II, M., Hall, D., Llinas, J.: Handbook of Multisensor Data Fusion: Theory and Practice. CRC Press, Boca Raton (2017)

23. Lippi, M., Mamei, M., Mariani, S., Zambonelli, F.: An argumentation-based perspective over the social IoT. IEEE Internet Things J., 1 (2017)

24. Lippi, M., Mamei, M., Mariani, S., Zambonelli, F.: Coordinating distributed speaking objects. In: 37th IEEE International Conference on Distributed Computing Systems, ICDCS 2017, Atlanta, USA, 5–8 June 2017
25. Maarala, A.I., Su, X., Riekki, J.: Semantic reasoning for context-aware internet of things applications. IEEE Internet Things J. **4**(2), 461–473 (2017)
26. Mariani, S.: Coordination of Complex Sociotechnical Systems - Self-organisation of Knowledge in MoK. Artificial Intelligence: Foundations, Theory, and Algorithms. Springer, Cham (2016). https://doi.org/10.1007/978-3-319-47109-9
27. Meneguzzi, F.R., Zorzo, A.F., da Costa Móra, M.: Propositional planning in BDI agents. In: Proceedings of the 2004 ACM Symposium on Applied Computing, SAC 2004, pp. 58–63. ACM, New York (2004)
28. Omicini, A., Viroli, M.: Coordination models and languages: from parallel computing to self-organisation. Knowl. Eng. Rev. **26**(1), 53–59 (2011)
29. Perera, C., Zaslavsky, A., Christen, P., Georgakopoulos, D.: Context aware computing for the internet of things: a survey. Commun. Surv. Tutorials **16**(1), 414–454 (2014)
30. Rahwan, I., Ramchurn, S.D., Jennings, N.R., Mcburney, P., Parsons, S., Sonenberg, L.: Argumentation-based negotiation. Knowl. Eng. Rev. **18**(4), 343–375 (2003)
31. Rao, A.S., Georgeff, M.P.: BDI agents: from theory to practice. In: Lesser, V.R., Gasser, L. (eds.) 1st International Conference on Multi Agent Systems (ICMAS 1995), pp. 312–319. The MIT Press, San Francisco, 12–14 June 1995
32. Razzaque, M.A., Milojevic-Jevric, M., Palade, A., Clarke, S.: Middleware for internet of things: a survey. IEEE Internet Things J. **3**(1), 70–95 (2016)
33. Roman, R., Zhou, J., Lopez, J.: On the features and challenges of security and privacy in distributed internet of things. Comput. Netw. **57**(10), 2266–2279 (2013)
34. Shi, W., Dustdar, S.: The promise of edge computing. Computer **49**(5), 78–81 (2016)
35. Tsai, C.-W., Lai, C.-F., Chiang, M.-C., Yang, L.T., et al.: Data mining for internet of things: a survey. IEEE Commun. Surv. Tutorials **16**(1), 77–97 (2014)
36. Walton, D., Krabbe, E.: Commitment in Dialogue: Basic Concept of Interpersonal Reasoning. State University of New York Press, Albany (1995)
37. Wooldridge, M.J.: Reasoning About Rational Agents. MIT press, Cambridge (2000)
38. Ye, J., Dobson, S., McKeever, S.: Situation identification techniques in pervasive computing: a review. Pervasive Mob. Comput. **8**(1), 36–66 (2012)
39. Yi, S., Li, C., Li, Q.: A survey of fog computing: concepts, applications and issues. In: Proceedings of the 2015 Workshop on Mobile Big Data, Mobidata 2015, pp. 37–42. ACM, New York (2015)
40. Zambonelli, F., Jennings, N.R., Wooldridge, M.: Developing multiagent systems: the Gaia methodology. ACM Trans. Softw. Eng. Methodol. **12**(3), 317–370 (2003)
41. Zambonelli, F., Salim, F., Loke, S.W., De Meuter, W., Kanhere, S.: Algorithmic governance in smart cities: the conundrum and the potential of pervasive computing solutions. IEEE Technol. Soc. Mag. **37**(2), 80–87 (2018)
42. Zambonelli, F., et al.: Developing pervasive multi-agent systems with nature-inspired coordination. Pervasive Mob. Comput. **17**(Part B), 236–252 (2015)
43. Zatelli, M.R., Hübner, J.F., Ricci, A., Bordini, R.H.: Conflicting goals in agent-oriented programming. In: Proceedings of the 6th International Workshop on Programming Based on Actors, Agents, and Decentralized Control, AGERE, pp. 21–30 (2016)

Injecting (Micro)Intelligence in the IoT: Logic-Based Approaches for (M)MAS

Andrea Omicini$^{(\boxtimes)}$ and Roberta Calegari

Dipartimento di Informatica — Scienza e Ingegneria (DISI),
Alma Mater Studiorum–Università di Bologna, Bologna, Italy
{andrea.omicini,roberta.calegari}@unibo.it

Abstract. Pervasiveness of ICT resources along with the promise of ubiquitous intelligence is pushing hard both our demand and our fears of AI: demand mandates for the ability to inject (micro) intelligence ubiquitously, fears compel the behaviour of intelligent systems to be observable, explainable, and accountable. Whereas the first wave of the new "AI Era" was mostly heralded by sub-symbolic approaches, features like explainability are better provided by symbolic techniques. In this paper we focus on logic-based approaches, and discuss their potential in pervasive scenarios like the IoT and open (M)MAS along with our latest results in the field.

Keywords: Pervasive system · MMAS · Micro-intelligence ·
Logic-based · LPaaS

1 Introduction

Human environment is more and more affected and even shaped by the increasing availability of ICT resources, in particular within the constantly-growing urban areas all over the world. The ubiquitous availability of personal devices, along with the increasing diffusion of sensor networks, actuator devices, and computational resources in general, is rapidly transforming urban environments into wannabe-smart environments on a massively-large scale.

Whereas model, technology, and methodology aspects are nowadays the subject of many research activities [47,48], the issue of (*ubiquitous*) *intelligence* is the key to make environment really smart. Many novel approaches to machine intelligence nowadays are increasingly focussing on *sub-symbolic* approaches – such as deep learning with neural neural networks, e.g., [42] – and how to make them work on the large scale. As promising as that may look – on the premise that those approaches have the potential minimise the engineering efforts towards large-scale intelligence – what we do also need is that our large-scale intelligent systems exhibit *socio-technical features* such as *observability*, *explanability*, and *accountability* to make ubiquitous intelligence actually work in human organisations and societies.

D. Lin et al. (Eds.): MMAS 2018, LNAI 11422, pp. 21–35, 2019.
https://doi.org/10.1007/978-3-030-20937-7_2

To this end, more classic AI approaches to intelligence can be of help—such as *agents* and *multi-agent systems* (MAS), as well as *declarative* and *logic-based* approaches. Agents are the most viable abstraction to encapsulate fundamental features such as *control, goals, mobility, intelligence* [48]. In particular, agents are widely recognised as the main abstractions to *distribute* intelligence in complex systems of any sort—e.g., [18]. Also, MAS abstractions such as *society* and *environment* [30] are essential to cope with the complexity of nowadays application scenarios—as well as to inject intelligence in complex computational systems [34].

On the other hand, declarative and logic-based technologies quite straightforwardly address issues such as *observability* and *explainability*, in particular when exploiting their inferential capabilities—e.g., [22]. Since logic-based approaches already have a well-understood role in building intelligent agents [40], we focus instead on the role that *logic-based* models and technologies can play when used to rule *agent societies* as well as to engineer *agent environment*.

In this paper we recap some of our research results about the role of logic-based models and technologies in MAS, discussing how they can be exploited to inject *micro-intelligence* [2] in large-scale scenarios. In particular, we show how Logic Programming as a Service (LPaaS [7]) can be used to distribute intelligence in KIE (knowledge-intensive environments), how Labelled Variables in Logic Programming (LVLP [4]) can help introducing *domain-specific* intelligence, and how the logic-based coordination language ReSpecT [32] can provide for social intelligence in MAS. Also, we show how logic-based approaches makes it possible to address in principle issues such as observability, formalisability, explainability, and accountability.

2   Background and Related Work

2.1   (M)MAS, IoT and Intelligence

Agent-oriented engineering and (massive) multi-agent systems – (M)MAS – have been already recognised as the most promising way for developing applications for the Internet of Things (IoT) as well as cyber-physical systems (CPS), since they are well-suited for supporting decentralised, loosely-coupled and highly dynamic, heterogeneous and open systems, in which components should be able to cooperate opportunistically [41]. Along that line, IoT and pervasive systems can be seen as (M)MAS, devoted to monitor and control our environments where the MAS abstractions, techniques, and methods are essential to cope with the complexity of the application scenarios. Several works (e.g., [24,28,43]) propose agents as the most natural way of approaching IoT systems featuring complexity, dynamism, situatedness, and autonomy. Moreover, agents are shown to be the most viable abstractions to encapsulate fundamental features such as control, goals, mobility and intelligence, in the development of proactive, cooperating, and context-aware smart objects [18].

In the following we focus our attention on the intelligence issue, a hot topic in current IoT research, following the idea that devices in IoT pervasive systems have to be massively networked and provided with (different degrees of) intelligence, in order to interoperate and cooperate to achieve different goals. To this end, agent-oriented models and technologies are gaining momentum for embedding decentralised intelligence—as discussed in [23].

2.2 Engineering Intelligence in the IoT: Key Challenges

The IoT extends the current Internet technology by connecting different types of things (objects, devices) with each other, and enable them to communicate *smartly* [46]. Consequently, the IoT concept is designed to connect millions of things together, yet things such a huge number need large storage spaces and generate heavy traffic, which potentially creates many network issues. Furthermore, while the things are connected with each other, they are not necessarily able to *communicate* meaningfully and *interoperate* effectively with each other [44]. Their ability to communicate with each other depends on the similarity of the service they are assigned to do [25]. Such deficiencies are due to the fact that simple computing things lack of the ability to reason on their environments and to subsequently make intelligent decisions and actions in order to achieve their objectives. Typically, the objects used in the IoT – e.g., RFID, sensors, televisions, washing machines, etc. – lacks intelligence due to hardware and software limitations.

In addition, the issues of security, governance and standardisation have to be taken in consideration [44]. No consolidated set of software engineering best practices has emerged so far in the IoT world [26,47] in order to face that issue: so, properly engineering such a new generation of scalable, highly-reactive, (often) resource-constrained software systems is still a challenge from the SE viewpoint.

Furthermore, *sociotechnical features* such as observability, explainability, and accountability have to be addressed whenever the complexity of automated reasoning goes far beyond the human ability to understand—and we are already there, basically. Understanding at some level how huge aggregates of intelligent devices and agents evolve and affect our social and organisation processes is to become essential for technical, social, normative, and ethical reasons. Apparently, there is where symbolic approaches like logic-based ones are going to be of help.

Along that line, in the following we focus on the practice of engineering and design intelligence in distributed systems, in particular in the IoT systems, by discussing our latest results in the field based on logic-based models and technologies.

3 Logic-Based Approaches for (M)MAS and IoT

In order to face the challenges and the open issues highlighted in Subsect. 2.2 we proposed a logic-based approach for injecting *micro-intelligence* in large-scale MAS, such as IoT pervasive systems.

Logic-based languages and technologies represent in principle a natural candidate for injecting intelligence within computational systems [1]: yet, many issues have to be addressed—among these, the computational costs, the machinery often not suited for programming in the large (the intrinsic modularity provided by predicates does not scale up effectively, and modules are not enough for the purpose), the "no-types" approach that makes it difficult to deal with domain-specific applications, the distance from mainstream programming paradigms, the integration with mainstream technologies. Moreover, MMAS and IoT inherently call for a fully distributed architecture, which is why the relationship between logic and physical distribution needs to be addressed and investigated in depth. Classical logic approaches apparently do not cope well with the current perception of distributed systems—for instance, the universal notion of consistency of the logic theory does not fit the incompleteness and inconsistency intrinsically implied by distributed scenarios.

Anyway, overall, we believe that a logic-based approach can bring some remarkable benefits in pervasive system, in particular dealing with the AI fears, by promoting observability, malleability, understandability, formalisability, and norm compliance—yet, a basic re-interpretation of some basic concepts of logic programming is clearly needed in order to cope well with the aforementioned issues.

Along with the re-interpretation of classical logic approach under the IoT vision, we define the concept of *micro-intelligence* [2]: small chunks of machine intelligence, spread all over the system, capable to enable the individual intelligence of any sort of devices, promoting coordination and interoperation among different entities. The micro-intelligence vision promotes the ubiquitous distribution of intelligence in large pervasive systems such as IoT ones, in particular when coupled with agent-based technologies and methods, at both the individual and the collective level—when combined with an overall architectural view of large-scale systems exploiting logic-based technologies. The idea behind micro-intelligence is that it can be encapsulated in devices of any sort, making them smart, as well as capable to work together in groups, aggregates, societies.

As a source of intelligence, we focus here on logic-based engines—in particular LP (logic programming) engines, offering inference capabilities spread all over the network. The potential of logic-based model and its extensions is first of all related to the observability and understandability of the entire system. Declarativeness and explicit knowledge representation of LP enable knowledge sharing at the most adequate level of abstraction, while supporting modularity and separation of concerns [29], which are specially valuable in open and dynamic distributed systems. As a further element, LP sound and complete semantics naturally enables intelligent agents to reason and infer new information in a sound way. Traditional LP has been proven to work well both as a knowledge representation language and as an inference platform for rational agents. Logic agents may interact with an external environment by means of a suitably defined observe–think–act cycle. Finally, LP extensions or logic-based computational models – such as meta-reasoning about situations [27] – could be incorporated so as to enable complex behaviours tailored to the situated components.

Accordingly, our result in the field are *(i)* the Logic Programming as a Service – LPaaS henceforth [7] – model for distributing logic programs and logic engines accordingly to the SOA architecture; *(ii)* the Labelled Variables in Logic Programming (LVLP henceforth [4]) extension to the LP model to answer the domain specificity issue of pervasive system; *(iii)* the possibility of exploiting logic-based coordination artefacts and logical tuples with the ReSpecT coordination language [32] upon the TuCSoN MAS coordination middleware [39].

In the following we shortly discuss each contribution, while trying to provide a general view of how logic-based models and technologies can be exploited to inject intelligence into (M)MAS.

4   LPaaS & LVLP for Environment Intelligence

4.1   Vision

The novel LPaaS & LVLP models and architectures – and the corresponding technology – express the concept of micro-intelligence defined above. In particular, we define two different, integrated models – namely, Logic Programming as a Service and Labelled Variables in Logic Programming – designed so as to act synergistically in order to support the distribution of intelligence in pervasive systems.

One one side, the LPaaS architecture is designed so that LP can act as a source of distributed intelligence for the IoT world, by providing an abstract view of LP inference engines in terms of service. It exploits the XaaS (everything as a service) metaphor to promote maximum availability and interoperability while promoting context-awareness: any resource of any sort should be accessible as a service (possibly an intelligent one) via standard network operations. From the MAS viewpoint, LPaaS takes care of distributing knowledge as well as reasoning capabilities in the agent environment based on LP.

On the other side, LVLP extends the LP model to enable diverse computational models, each tailored to a specific situated component, to coherently and fruitfully coexist and cooperate within the same (logic-based) framework, so as to cope with *domain-specific* aspects. From the MAS viewpoint, LVLP takes care of embedding domain specific knowledge and reasoning capabilities at the micro-level [48].

The added value of such a hybrid approach is to make it possible to exploit LP for what it is most suited for – such as symbolic computation –, while delegating other aspects – such as situated computation – to other most suitable languages or computational levels.

4.2   LPaaS in a Nutshell

The LPaaS has been introduced in [5,6]. A detailed discussion on the technology can be found in [3], whereas a comprehensive account was presented in [7].

The main idea behind LPaaS is to embed a (possibly situated) logic theory in every computational device composing the MAS environment, along with a working logic engine providing the system with basic inferential capabilities. Multiple theories are intended to be consistent under the fundamental assumption that each logic theory describes axiomatically what is locally true—so, preventing logical inconsistency a priori. So, agents exploit both knowledge representation provided by logic theories and the inferential capabilities provided by logic engines as a distributed service, injecting intelligence in MAS environment.

To do so, LPaaS promote a radical re-interpretation of some basic facets of LP, moving LP towards the notion of *situated service*. Such a notion articulates along four major aspects: *(i)* the preservation (with re-contextualisation) of the SLD resolution process; *(ii)* stateless interactions; *(iii)* time-sensitive computations; *(iv)* space-sensitive computations. The SLD resolution process remains a staple in LPaaS: yet, it is re-contextualised in the situated nature of the specific LP service. This means that, given the precise *spatial*, *temporal*, and *general* contexts within which the service is operating *when the resolution process starts*, the process follows the usual rules of SLD resolution: situatedness is accounted for through the service abstraction with respect to such three contexts.

From an architectural viewpoint, *service-oriented architecture* (SOA) nowadays represents the standard approach for distributed system engineering: so, LPaaS adopts the *Software as a Service* architecture as its architectural reference [14]. Moreover, LP services in LPaaS can be fruitfully interpreted as *microservices* [17].

Accordingly, the LPaaS abstraction represents a form of micro-intelligence, enabling situated reasoning, interaction, and coordination in distributed systems, as the process by which an entity is able reason about its local actions and the (anticipated) actions of others so as to try and ensure the community acts in a coherent manner. LPaaS means to empower reasoning in distributed systems taking into account the explicit definition of the spatio-temporal structure of the environment where situated entities act and interact, thus exploiting the inner nature of pervasive systems while promoting environment awareness.

4.3 LVLP in a Nutshell

Specificity of local domains, however, might not be easily addressed by the general-purpose approach of standard LP—in terms of both specific domain knowledge and domain-specific inference. For instance, the typical LP language, Prolog, is even untyped—which, roughly speaking, is good for generality, bad for making applications domain specific.

To this end, specific domain intelligence can be injected in MAS environment via Labelled Variables in Logic Programming, formally discussed in [4] and fully developed in [4]. Basically, the LVLP approach is consistent with that part of AI literature that has established that domain-specific knowledge is a major determinant of the success of KIE systems such as expert systems [13].

LVLP builds upon the general notion of *label* as defined by Gabbay [19], and adopts the techniques introduced by Holzbaur [21] to develop a generalisation of

LP where labels are exploited to define computations in domain-specific contexts. LVLP allows heterogeneous devices in large-scale applications to have specific application goals and manage specific sorts of information, enabling reactivity to environment change while capturing diverse logic and domains exploiting the concept of *labelled variable.*

An LVLP program is a collection of rules. LVLP *rules* have the form *Head ←Labelling, Body*, to be read as *"Head if Body given Labelling"*. There, *Head* is an atomic formula, *Labelling* is the list of labelled variables in the clause, and *Body* is a list of atomic formulas. By design, only variables can be labelled in LVLP. Given two generic LVLP terms, the unification result is represented by the extended tuple $(true/false, \theta, \ell)$ where *true/false* represents the existence of an answer, θ is the *most general unifier (mgu)*, and ℓ is the new label associated to the unified variables defined by the user defined (label-)combining function. The unification process is extended by two functions: namely, the (label-)*combining function* exploited during the unification of two labelled variables, and the *compatibility function* exploited during the unification between a ground term and a labelled variable, ensuring the term is compatible with the label of the variable when interpreted in the domain of labels.

Among the many differences w.r.t. the approaches in the state of the art is the fact that our approach does not change the basic of the logic language, which remains the same, but allows for different specific extensions tailored to local needs. Overall, the main idea behind LVLP is to enable diverse computational models via labelled variables: each logic engine can exploit its own local label systems tailored to the specific needs of situated components, to coherently and fruitfully coexist side by side, interacting within a logic-based framework.

4.4 LPaaS & LVLP in (M)MAS

In [8] we discuss how the LPaaS architecture can be exploited to inject micro-intelligence in MAS, by enriching the overall MAS architecture with the notion of LPaaS agent/service, which allows for situated reasoning on locally-available data by design. The LPaaS model can be further extended towards domain-specific computations via LVLP.

As mentioned above, the multi-agent paradigm offers a powerful mechanism for *autonomous* and *situated* behaviour, supporting *social* and *cooperative* exchanges within *organisations* that are required for large-scale systems. Besides autonomy, situatedness, and sociality, large-scale application scenarios such as the IoT may benefit from other agent features – e.g., *mobility* and *intelligence* – that could straightforwardly map onto the multitude of heterogeneous devices. However, whereas mobility may come at a reasonable cost, intelligence is considerably a more challenging issue, in particular when computationally expensive technologies – such as machine learning, common-sense reasoning, natural language processing, advanced situation recognition and context awareness – are involved. Along this line, whenever local agent intelligence cannot be available for any reason – i.e. memory constraints hindering the opportunity to have a local KB, CPU constraints limiting efficiency of reasoning, etc. – a given agent may

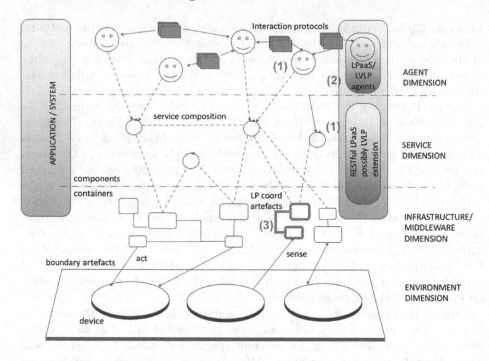

Fig. 1. Overview of a LPaaS-LVLP MAS

simply request to another, "more intelligent" one, to perform some intelligent activity on its behalf.

More interestingly here, intelligent activity could be also delegated to the environment—for instance, relying on LPaaS-LVLP services instead of the agents. In such a scenario, agents are always computationally efficient and responsive, since they are able to delegate reasoning-related tasks – such as situation recognition, planning, inference of novel information, etc. – to dedicated infrastructural services based on LPaaS-LVLP.

Figure 1 illustrates the model of the LPaaS-LVLP approach depicting the whole picture where *(1)* some agents are designed as lightweight ones, and rely on infrastructural services (or other more "intelligent" agents) to get LPaaS functionalities; *(2)* some agents embed the LPaaS-LVLP functionalities; *(3)* some LP functionalities are embedded in some services provided by the middleware (namely, by the containers). In particular, at the bottom layer, the physical/computational environment lives, with *boundary artefacts* [35] taking care of its representation and interactions with the rest of the MAS. Then, typically, some middleware infrastructure provides common API and services to application-level software – i.e., the containers where service components live – there including the *coordination artefacts* [35] governing the interaction space. Finally, on top of the middleware, the application/system as a whole lives, viewed as a mixture of services and agents.

5   ReSpecT and Logical Tuples for Social Intelligence

5.1   Vision

In general, *coordination artefact* [37] are meant to encapsulate coordination policies for distributed systems, so as to inject *social intelligence* within computational systems [9]. By designing them as *observable*, coordination artefacts have the potential to make social intelligence potentially *explainable*. By designing them as *malleable*, coordination artefacts can make social intelligence *adaptable* [36]. In particular, *logic-based coordination artefacts* could in principle be exploited to represent coordination policies in a declarative way, and also possibly pave the way towards (partial) *formalisation* of large-scale systems.

In the context of MAS, social intelligence is another dimension that agent-based models and technologies can fruitfully exploit—in particular by building agent societies around *programmable, observable* and *malleable* coordination abstractions [35]. This is in fact the role of *coordination* models and technologies [10], where *coordination media* are the basic abstractions around which agent societies can be designed [11].

Agents and MAS are typically provided with coordination media via *coordination middleware* [12]: there, a multiplicity of distributed coordination media are made available to the MAS so that each group of agents can interact within a shared environment via a locally-deployed coordination medium The notion of *coordination as a service* expresses precisely that: autonomous agents submit themselves to the coordination policies embedded in a coordination medium by choosing to interact with other agents through the medium itself, thus constituting an *agent society* [45].

5.2   TuCSoN and ReSpecT in a Nutshell

The TuCSoN coordination model [39] provides MAS with *tuple centres* [32] that extend LINDA tuple spaces [20] with *programmability* [15] based on the ReSpecT [31] logic-based language. In particular, ReSpecT tuple centres contain *logic tuples* in the tuple space, and ReSpecT *specification tuples* in the *specification space*, which sets the coordinative behaviour of the medium by defining the *reaction* of the tuple centres to relevant MAS events.

More precisely, a ReSpecT specification tuple is a special kind of first-order logic tuple of the form reaction(E,G,R), where: E is the *triggering event* of the reaction, that is, the coordination-related event – represented by the coordination primitive invoked – whose occurrence triggers evaluation of the *reaction*; G is the (set of) *guard predicate*(s) which must evaluate to true for the reaction to actually execute—enabling fine-grained control over reactions execution; R is the *reaction body*, that is, the set of Prolog computations and ReSpecT primitives to execute to bring about the reaction effects.

Whereas the ReSpecT tuple space contains the (logic) tuples used for the *communication* among agents, the ReSpecT specification space contains the (logic) specification tuples used for the *coordination* of agents. So, ReSpecT tuple centres exploit logic for both knowledge representation (in the communication space) and coordination policies (in the coordination space) in agent societies.

Overall, ReSpecT tuple centres are *programmable* – via ReSpecT specification tuples –, *observable* – in that both the basic and the specification tuples can be accessed by the agents – and *malleable*—in that suitable specification primitives can be used to change the ReSpecT behaviour specification at runtime. Programmability of the coordination medium – along with the Turing-equivalence of ReSpecT [16] – makes it possible to embed any computable coordination policy within the coordination media, possibly allowing for *intelligent social behaviour*—e.g., [33]. Observability of all tuples in a tuple centre makes it possible to reason about the state and behaviour of the corresponding agent society. Malleability of the tuple centre behaviour makes it possible to *change* the (possibly intelligent) coordinative behaviour at run-time, thus paving the way towards *adaptability*.

Moreover, a typical feature of tuple-based middleware – which clearly fits large-scale scenarios – is the multiplicity of distributed coordination media made available to the MAS: each group of agents can interact within a shared environment via a locally-deployed coordination medium. Along this line, TuCSoN middleware supports multiple ReSpecT tuple centres, which can be spatially distributed and connected via *linkability* [38]. Accordingly, ReSpecT tuple centres can be designed to be locally deployed within a physically-distributed environment, with a (possibly huge) number of spatial containers and physical devices, and correspondingly embodying the laws for *local* coordination, ruling the social behaviour of the locally-interacting agents. Any coordination policy can then be tailored to the specific needs of every locality in a large-scale scenario—thus providing a way towards *scalable coordination*.

6   Conclusion

When properly integrated within agent-based models and technologies, logic-based approaches have the potential to be exploited for knowledge representation and reasoning at the large scale. In this invited paper we intentionally ignore the role of logic within agents, by focussing instead on how logic-based models can be exploited to inject *micro-intelligence* through agent *societies* and MAS *environment*. By adopting LPaaS, LVLP, and ReSpecT as our reference logic-based models and technologies, we discuss their potential impact upon large-scale MAS for complex application scenarios such as the IoT.

Altogether, the logic-based approaches discussed in this paper can lead to the overall architecture depicted in Fig. 2. There,

– distributed logic engines augment MAS environment with widespread *micro-intelligence*
– exploited as standard *services* by components of any sorts, including intelligent agents via LPaaS
– possibly enhanced as situated and *domain-specific* extensions via LVLP

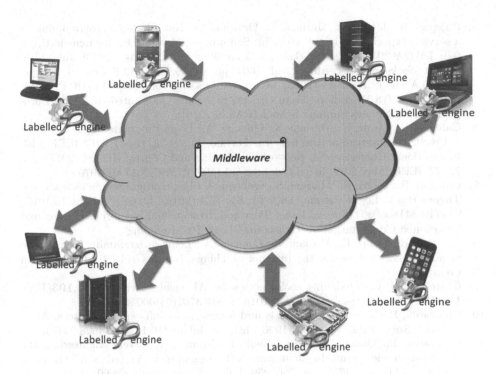

Fig. 2. Overview LPaaS-LVLP-ReSpecT MAS architecture

- coordinated via ReSpecT logic-based artefacts, encapsulating *social intelligence*
- based on a logic-based *middleware* like TuCSoN

In the end, whereas sub-symbolic approaches to AI are currently taking the stage – especially in the eye of the public opinion – symbolic approaches, yet with a long road ahead, still have the potential to be key players in the future of large-scale intelligent systems.

References

1. Brownlee, J.: Clever Algorithms: Nature-inspired Programming Recipes (2011)
2. Calegari, R.: Micro-intelligence for the IoT: logic-based models and technologies. Ph.D. thesis, Alma Mater Studiorum—Università di Bologna, Bologna, Italy (2018). https://doi.org/10.6092/unibo/amsdottorato/8521
3. Calegari, R., Ciatto, G., Mariani, S., Denti, E., Omicini, A.: Micro-intelligence for the IoT: SE challenges and practice in LPaaS. In: 2018 IEEE International Conference on Cloud Engineering (IC2E 208), 17–20 April 2018, pp. 292–297. IEEE Computer Society (2018). https://doi.org/10.1109/IC2E.2018.00061
4. Calegari, R., Denti, E., Dovier, A., Omicini, A.: Extending logic programming with labelled variables: model and semantics. Fundam. Inform. **161**, 53–74 (2018). https://doi.org/10.3233/FI-2018-1695. Special Issue CILC 2016

5. Calegari, R., Denti, E., Mariani, S., Omicini, A.: Towards logic programming as a service: experiments in tuProlog. In: Santoro, C., Messina, F., De Benedetti, M. (eds.) WOA 2016 – 17th Workshop "From Objects to Agents", 29–30 July 2016. CEUR Workshop Proceedings, vol. 1664, pp. 91–99. Sun SITE Central Europe, RWTH Aachen University (2016). http://ceur-ws.org/Vol-1664/w14.pdf, Proceedings of the 17th Workshop "From Objects to Agents" co-located with 18th European Agent Systems Summer School (EASSS 2016)
6. Calegari, R., Denti, E., Mariani, S., Omicini, A.: Logic Programming as a Service (LPaaS): intelligence for the IoT. In: Fortino, G., et al. (eds.) 2017 IEEE 14th International Conference on Networking, Sensing and Control (ICNSC 2017), pp. 72–77. IEEE, May 2017. https://doi.org/10.1109/ICNSC.2017.8000070
7. Calegari, R., Denti, E., Mariani, S., Omicini, A.: Logic programming as a service. Theory Pract. Log. Program. 18(5–6), 846–873 (2018). https://doi.org/10.1017/S1471068418000364. Special Issue "Past and Present (and Future) of Parallel and Distributed Computation in (Constraint) Logic Programming"
8. Calegari, R., Denti, E., Mariani, S., Omicini, A.: Logic programming as a service in multi-agent systems for the Internet of Things. Int. J. Grid Util. Comput. (in press)
9. Castelfranchi, C.: Modelling social action for AI agents. Artif. Intell. 103(1–2), 157–182 (1998). https://doi.org/10.1016/S0004-3702(98)00056-3
10. Ciancarini, P.: Coordination models and languages as software integrators. ACM Comput. Surv. 28(2), 300–302 (1996). https://doi.org/10.1145/234528.234732
11. Ciancarini, P., Omicini, A., Zambonelli, F.: Multiagent system engineering: the coordination viewpoint. In: Jennings, N.R., Lespérance, Y. (eds.) ATAL 1999. LNCS (LNAI), vol. 1757, pp. 250–259. Springer, Heidelberg (2000). https://doi.org/10.1007/10719619_19
12. Ciatto, G., Mariani, S., Omicini, A., Zambonelli, F., Louvel, M.: Twenty years of coordination technologies: state-of-the-art and perspectives. In: Di Marzo Serugendo, G., Loreti, M. (eds.) COORDINATION 2018. LNCS, vol. 10852, pp. 51–80. Springer, Cham (2018). https://doi.org/10.1007/978-3-319-92408-3_3
13. Crevier, D.: AI: The Tumultuous History of the Search for Artificial Intelligence. Basic Books, New York (1993)
14. Cusumano, M.: Cloud computing and SaaS as new computing platforms. Commun. ACM 53(4), 27–29 (2010). https://doi.org/10.1145/1721654.1721667
15. Denti, E., Natali, A., Omicini, A.: Programmable coordination media. In: Garlan, D., Le Métayer, D. (eds.) COORDINATION 1997. LNCS, vol. 1282, pp. 274–288. Springer, Heidelberg (1997). https://doi.org/10.1007/3-540-63383-9_86
16. Denti, E., Natali, A., Omicini, A.: On the expressive power of a language for programming coordination media. In: 1998 ACM Symposium on Applied Computing (SAC 1998), Atlanta, GA, USA, 27 February–1 March 1998, pp. 169–177. ACM, New York (1998). https://doi.org/10.1145/330560.330665. Special Track on Coordination Models, Languages and Applications
17. Familiar, B.: Microservices, IoT, and Azure: Leveraging DevOps and Microservice Architecture to Deliver SaaS Solutions, 1st edn. Apress, Berkely (2015)
18. Fortino, G., Guerrieri, A., Russo, W.: Agent-oriented smart objects development. In: 2012 IEEE 16th International Conference on Computer Supported Cooperative Work in Design (CSCWD 2012), pp. 907–912. IEEE, May 2012. https://doi.org/10.1109/CSCWD.2012.6221929
19. Gabbay, D.M.: Labelled Deductive Systems, vol. 1. Oxford Logic Guides, vol. 33. Clarendon Press, Oxford (1996). http://global.oup.com/academic/product/labelled-deductive-systems-9780198538332

20. Gelernter, D.: Generative communication in Linda. ACM Trans. Program. Lang. Syst. **7**(1), 80–112 (1985). https://doi.org/10.1145/2363.2433
21. Holzbaur, C.: Metastructures vs. attributed variables in the context of extensible unification. In: Bruynooghe, M., Wirsing, M. (eds.) PLILP 1992. LNCS, vol. 631, pp. 260–268. Springer, Heidelberg (1992). https://doi.org/10.1007/3-540-55844-6_141
22. Idelberger, F., Governatori, G., Riveret, R., Sartor, G.: Evaluation of logic-based smart contracts for blockchain systems. In: Alferes, J.J., Bertossi, L., Governatori, G., Fodor, P., Roman, D. (eds.) RuleML 2016. LNCS, vol. 9718, pp. 167–183. Springer, Cham (2016). https://doi.org/10.1007/978-3-319-42019-6_11
23. Jamont, J.P., Occello, M.: Meeting the challenges of decentralised embedded applications using multi-agent systems. Int. J. Agent-Oriented Softw. Eng. **5**(1), 22–68 (2016). https://doi.org/10.1504/IJAOSE.2015.078435
24. Kato, T., Chiba, R., Takahashi, H., Kinoshita, T.: Agent-oriented cooperation of IoT devices towards advanced logistics. In: 2015 IEEE 39th Annual Computer Software and Applications Conference (COMPSACW 2015), vol. 3, pp. 223–227, July 2015. https://doi.org/10.1109/COMPSAC.2015.237
25. Khan, R., Khan, S.U., Zaheer, R., Khan, S.: Future internet: the Internet of Things architecture, possible applications and key challenges. In: 10th International Conference on Frontiers of Information Technology (FIT 2012), pp. 257–260, December 2012. https://doi.org/10.1109/FIT.2012.53
26. Larrucea, X., Combelles, A., Favaro, J., Taneja, K.: Software engineering for the Internet of Things. IEEE Softw. **34**(1), 24–28 (2017). https://doi.org/10.1109/MS.2017.28
27. Loke, S.W.: Representing and reasoning with situations for context-aware pervasive computing: a logic programming perspective. Knowl. Eng. Rev. **19**(3), 213–233 (2004). https://doi.org/10.1017/S0269888905000263
28. Manzalini, A., Zambonelli, F.: Towards autonomic and situation-aware communication services: the CASCADAS vision. In: IEEE Workshop on Distributed Intelligent Systems: Collective Intelligence and Its Applications (DIS 2006), pp. 383–388, June 2006. https://doi.org/10.1109/DIS.2006.71
29. Oliya, M., Pung, H.K.: Towards incremental reasoning for context aware systems. In: Abraham, A., Lloret Mauri, J., Buford, J.F., Suzuki, J., Thampi, S.M. (eds.) ACC 2011, Part I. CCIS, vol. 190, pp. 232–241. Springer, Heidelberg (2011). https://doi.org/10.1007/978-3-642-22709-7_24
30. Omicini, A.: SODA: societies and infrastructures in the analysis and design of agent-based systems. In: Ciancarini, P., Wooldridge, M.J. (eds.) AOSE 2000. LNCS, vol. 1957, pp. 185–193. Springer, Heidelberg (2001). https://doi.org/10.1007/3-540-44564-1_12
31. Omicini, A.: Formal ReSpecT in the A&A perspective. Electron. Notes Theor. Comput. Sci. **175**(2), 97–117 (2007). https://doi.org/10.1016/j.entcs.2007.03.006. 5th International Workshop on Foundations of Coordination Languages and Software Architectures (FOCLASA 2006), CONCUR 2006, Bonn, Germany, 31 August 2006. Post-proceedings
32. Omicini, A., Denti, E.: From tuple spaces to tuple centres. Sci. Comput. Program. **41**(3), 277–294 (2001). https://doi.org/10.1016/S0167-6423(01)00011-9
33. Omicini, A., Denti, E., Natali, A.: Agent coordination and control through logic theories. In: Gori, M., Soda, G. (eds.) AI*IA 1995. LNCS, vol. 992, pp. 439–450. Springer, Heidelberg (1995). https://doi.org/10.1007/3-540-60437-5_43

34. Omicini, A., Mariani, S.: Agents & multiagent systems: en route towards complex intelligent systems. Intell. Artif. **7**(2), 153–164 (2013). https://doi.org/10.3233/IA-130056. Special Issue Celebrating 25 years of the Italian Association for Artificial Intelligence

35. Omicini, A., Ricci, A., Viroli, M.: Agens Faber: toward a theory of artefacts for MAS. Electron. Notes Theor. Comput. Sci. **150**(3), 21–36 (2006). https://doi.org/10.1016/j.entcs.2006.03.003

36. Omicini, A., Ricci, A., Viroli, M.: Artifacts in the A&A meta-model for multi-agent systems. Auton. Agents Multi-Agent Syst. **17**(3), 432–456 (2008). https://doi.org/10.1007/s10458-008-9053-x. Special Issue on Foundations, Advanced Topics and Industrial Perspectives of Multi-Agent Systems

37. Omicini, A., Ricci, A., Viroli, M., Castelfranchi, C., Tummolini, L.: Coordination artifacts: environment-based coordination for intelligent agents. In: Jennings, N.R., Sierra, C., Sonenberg, L., Tambe, M. (eds.) 3rd International Joint Conference on Autonomous Agents and Multiagent Systems (AAMAS 2004), vol. 1, pp. 286–293. ACM, New York, 19–23 July 2004. https://doi.org/10.1109/AAMAS.2004.10070

38. Omicini, A., Ricci, A., Zaghini, N.: Distributed workflow upon linkable coordination artifacts. In: Ciancarini, P., Wiklicky, H. (eds.) COORDINATION 2006. LNCS, vol. 4038, pp. 228–246. Springer, Heidelberg (2006). https://doi.org/10.1007/11767954_15

39. Omicini, A., Zambonelli, F.: Coordination for Internet application development. Auton. Agents Multi-Agent Syst. **2**(3), 251–269 (1999). https://doi.org/10.1023/A:1010060322135. Special Issue: Coordination Mechanisms for Web Agents

40. Omicini, A., Zambonelli, F.: MAS as complex systems: a view on the role of declarative approaches. In: Leite, J., Omicini, A., Sterling, L., Torroni, P. (eds.) DALT 2003. LNCS (LNAI), vol. 2990, pp. 1–16. Springer, Heidelberg (2004). https://doi.org/10.1007/978-3-540-25932-9_1

41. Savaglio, C., Fortino, G., Ganzha, M., Paprzycki, M., Bădică, C., Ivanović, M.: Agent-based computing in the Internet of Things: a survey. In: Ivanović, M., Bădică, C., Dix, J., Jovanović, Z., Malgeri, M., Savić, M. (eds.) IDC 2017. SCI, vol. 737, pp. 307–320. Springer, Cham (2018). https://doi.org/10.1007/978-3-319-66379-1_27

42. Silver, D., et al.: Mastering the game of Go with deep neural networks and tree search. Nature **529**, 484–489 (2016). https://doi.org/10.1038/nature16961

43. Spanoudakis, N., Moraitis, P.: Engineering ambient intelligence systems using agent technology. IEEE Intell. Syst. **30**(3), 60–67 (2015). https://doi.org/10.1109/MIS.2015.3

44. Tan, L., Wang, N.: Future internet: the Internet of Things. In: 3rd International Conference on Advanced Computer Theory and Engineering (ICACTE 2010), vol. 5, pp. V376–V380, August 2010. https://doi.org/10.1109/ICACTE.2010.5579543

45. Viroli, M., Omicini, A.: Coordination as a service. Fundam. Inform. **73**(4), 507–534 (2006). http://content.iospress.com/articles/fundamenta-informaticae/fi73-4-04. Special Issue: Best papers of FOCLASA 2002

46. Xiang, C., Li, X.: General analysis on architecture and key technologies about Internet of Things. In: IEEE International Conference on Computer Science and Automation Engineering (CSAE 2012), pp. 325–328, June 2012. https://doi.org/10.1109/ICSESS.2012.6269471

47. Zambonelli, F.: Key abstractions for IoT-oriented software engineering. IEEE Softw. **34**(1), 38–45 (2017). https://doi.org/10.1109/MS.2017.3
48. Zambonelli, F., Omicini, A.: Challenges and research directions in agent-oriented software engineering. Auton. Agents Multi-Agent Syst. **9**(3), 253–283 (2004). https://doi.org/10.1023/B:AGNT.0000038028.66672.1e. Special Issue: Challenges for Agent-Based Computing

Integrating Internet of Services and Internet of Things from a Multiagent Perspective

Donghui Lin[1]($\boxtimes$), Yohei Murakami[2], and Toru Ishida[1]

[1] Department of Social Informatics, Kyoto University, Yoshida Honmachi,
Sakyo, Kyoto 606-8501, Japan
{lindh,ishida}@i.kyoto-u.ac.jp
[2] Graduate School of Information Science and Engineering, Ritsumeikan University,
1-1-1 Noji-higashi, Kusatsu, Shiga 525-8577, Japan
yohei@fc.ritsumei.ac.jp

Abstract. To realize the Internet-based sociotechnical systems, it is necessary to build a comprehensive and effective infrastructure to support the interaction between various cloud services on the Internet and the physical world in which we live. For example, the information produced by the sensors is usually aggregated, processed and analyzed by services in the cloud, which can be used by various stakeholders for decision-making in many different application fields. Therefore, we need to consider integrating the Internet of Services (IoS), which enables the flexible sharing and composition of cloud services on the Internet, with the Internet of Things (IoT), which represents the constellation of things equipped with various sensors and actuators. The integration of IoS and IoT often involves multiple parties and so must deal with complex issues such as interaction, dynamics, scalability and decision making, all of which can be studied from a multiagent perspective. In this paper, we start by discussing the necessities and challenges for integrating IoS and IoT. Then, we propose an integrated architecture and examine it from two multiagent perspectives. One is to regard the integrated architecture of IoS and IoT as a multiagent-based architecture considering various patterns of service composition and interaction. The other is to apply multiagent methodologies when designing sociotechnical systems for various application domains based on the integrated IoS/IoT architecture. Moreover, we use the example application of designing multilingual environments to discuss the above two perspectives with possible future research directions.

Keywords: Internet of Things · Internet of Services ·
Sociotechnical systems · Multiagent systems

1 Introduction

The service-oriented architecture (SOA) is considered to be a key concept in the Internet of Services (IoS), which enables service providers to deploy data,

© Springer Nature Switzerland AG 2019
D. Lin et al. (Eds.): MMAS 2018, LNAI 11422, pp. 36–49, 2019.
https://doi.org/10.1007/978-3-030-20937-7_3

software and business processes as Web services or cloud services on the Internet [34]. Infrastructures based on SOA help service users create various real-world applications easily by invoking and composing available cloud services. A typical example of SOA usage is the Language Grid; it supports the sharing and creation of various types of language services on the Internet by encouraging service users to develop customized multi-language communication tools and intercultural collaboration environments [16]. On the other hand, the emergence of Internet of Things (IoT) in recent years has enabled things to be connected on the Internet. Things in the IoT environments are monitored and controlled by sensors and actuators [41]. The information collected by the IoT devices can be analyzed and used for making decisions as well as triggering cloud services instantiated on the IoS. IoS-based cloud services can also trigger sensors and actuators in IoT environments.

To enable the easy development and deployment of application systems that employ various cloud services on the Internet and things in the physical world, it is necessary to build an integrated infrastructure to support interaction between them. There are, however, several barriers to the integration of IoS and IoT; key issues are extreme heterogeneity, ultra-large scale, and the dynamic nature [17]. First, the extreme heterogeneity of cloud services and things renders service composition based on the traditional SOA rather inefficient due to the issue of interoperability. We need to deal with the interoperability of the cloud services in the IoS infrastructure and things in the IoT environment. Second, the ultra-large scale of cloud services and things negatively impact the performance of any integrated architecture of IoS and IoT. Third, it is necessary to realize new mechanisms for service composition that can deal with dynamic changes in the availability of cloud services and things, as well as the user's situation. Moreover, the application systems based on IoS and IoT, which can be regarded as Internet-based sociotechnical systems, always involve multiple stakeholders and so are difficult to design.

Since the integration of IoS and IoT involves a complex social process of service composition with important issues of interaction, dynamics, scalability, heterogeneity and decision making, it can be considered from a perspective of a multiagent system, which is composed of a set of agents that perform complicated tasks by negotiation and cooperation [47–49]. The multiagent perspective has already been used to investigate and interpret many existing systems such as sensor networks [4], social networks [19] and crowdsourcing systems [18], which will also be useful to explore effective methodologies for understanding behaviors of various stakeholders and modeling comprehensive sociotechnical systems built based on the integration of IoS and IoT.

In this paper, we propose an integrated architecture of IoS and IoT by using the Language Grid as an example of IoS infrastructure. In the framework, we mainly focus on the components for service composition based on cloud services on IoS and things on IoT. Then we describe the proposed framework from a multiagent perspective while emphasizing two specific aspects: architecture integration and application design. We discuss the possibility of developing the integrated architecture of IoS and IoT as a multiagent-based architecture and applying multiagent methodologies for designing sociotechnical systems based on the integrated architecture. In this sense, we are not aiming to propose a new agent framework for IoS/IoT integration in this paper; rather we try to understand important issues and key concepts of the integration from the viewpoint of multiagent systems.

The rest of this paper is organized as follows: In Sect. 2, we provide the background of IoS and IoT, and then introduce the issues for integrating IoS and IoT in Sect. 3. Section 4 describes a multiagent perspective for the integration of IoS and IoT from two different aspects. Section 5 provides an example application of multilingual environment design. Finally, the conclusion is presented in the last section.

2   Background of IoS and IoT

2.1   Internet of Services (IoS)

The Internet of Services (IoS) can be explained in different ways depending on the different definitions of services. In the research area of service-oriented computing (SOC), services are usually defined as "self-describing, platform-agnostic computational elements that support rapid, low-cost composition of distributed applications [35]."

Service-oriented architecture (SOA) is a key concept to realize the IoS [37], where software, data or business processes are deployed as Web services by service providers and used by service clients or service users. In SOA, there are basic services or atomic services that provide single functions of software or operations of data, as well as composite services composed by multiple atomic services to realize complicated functions or operations. Web services are evaluated by Quality of Services (QoS), the metrics of which include several non-functional attributes including cost, response time, availability, throughput, reputation and so on [50]. Therefore, QoS-aware service selection and service composition are essential technologies for IoS realization, which have been widely studied in the research area of SOC.

IoS has already been discussed a lot from the multiagent perspective [12,43]. Service-oriented systems have been said to realize many of the ideas generated in the research of multiagent systems. The multiagent-based SOC research challenges proposed involve pervasive service environments, society-inspired systems, and computational service mechanisms [13]. Moreover, interaction protocols in multiagent systems were applied for SOA in previous research and realized as a commitment-based SOA [42].

Since IoS involves various services and stakeholders, it can be regarded as a sociotechnical system where interaction between people and technology frequently occurs. We adopted the sociotechnical approach [8,40] to develop the Language Grid, an IoS infrastructure for language services [16]. The Language

Grid is a multilingual service infrastructure for supporting multi-language communication and intercultural collaboration activities, and enables easy registration and sharing of various language resources such as online dictionaries, bilingual corpora, morphological analyzers, and machine translators [14,27]. The concept of the Language Grid is to address the language resource interoperability by defining and implementing standardized language service interfaces for service composition and customization. The Language Grid was used in our previous studies on QoS-aware service composition and recommendation [10,26], combination of human services and Web services [23], and policy-aware service execution [46].

2.2 Internet of Things (IoT)

The Internet of Things (IoT) fuses things with the Internet to enable easy integration of the physical world into cyberspaces [2]. IoT is regarded as a key infrastructure in various application domains including the smart home, smart city, smart factory, healthcare, transportation, agriculture and so on. Typical enabling technologies in IoT include sensors and actuators, which are used to monitor and control things in the real world. The information produced by things in the IoT environments can be processed by cloud services and used by various stakeholders for decision-making in their application domains. Therefore, the technologies key to enabling current IoT-based applications include collecting, processing and analyzing information from things, and making decisions from the processed information. Since the information from IoT devices is regarded as big data in many situations, advanced machine learning technologies are often applied for analyzing such data. Moreover, high performance computing environments are necessary to handle IoT big data for ensuring real-time processing in various application domains.

Since IoT is an emerging idea, its architecture, enabling technologies, protocols and standards are being widely discussed from different perspectives. Identification, sensing, communication, computation, service and semantics are seen as key IoT elements, while big data analytics, cloud computing, high performance computing and fog computing are regarded as supporting technologies for IoT in a previous study [2]. IoT was also studied from an SOC perspective, where the IoT architecture was described as consisting of sensing layer, networking layer, service layer and interface layer [9]. However, IoT faces many challenging issues related to Quality of Services (QoS) including availability, reliability, mobility, performance, scalability, security, management, and trust. Interoperability is another important issue considering the heterogeneity of IoT device types and specifications.

IoT has also been studied from a multiagent perspective, where an IoT-enabled application is regarded as a social process involving multiple autonomous parties making it possible to be realized as decentralized multiagent systems [41]. Moreover, decentralization, asynchrony and decoupled enactment, governance of security, accountability and privacy were summarized as several important elements of IoT. Further, possible research directions in decentralized MAS has been proposed including programming models, interaction-oriented software engineering and enlightened governance. Since there are a large amount of devices connected in the environment, massively multiagent systems could be a promising design paradigm for IoT.

3   Issues for Integrating IoS and IoT

To build Internet-based sociotechnical systems like the multilingual environments, we are focused on the technologies needed to compose cloud services for IoS environments. With the development of IoT infrastructure and the availability of various sensors and actuators, it has become possible to provide high-quality services to users by satisfying their requirements in various situations. For example, sensors can be used to detect users' situational information like user interests and degree of satisfaction with a multilingual interactive agent. Based on this situational information, customized atomic services and composite services in the IoS can be provided to users in different situations. Therefore, it is important to consider integrating IoS and IoT for sociotechnical systems. However, there are several issues that we need to consider when integrating IoS and IoT. Previous research in the SOC field has studied how the SOA paradigm may be revisited to address the challenges posed by IoT, i.e. extreme heterogeneity, ultra-large scale, and dynamic changes [17]. These IoT challenges greatly impact the integration of IoS and IoT.

First, the extreme heterogeneity of IoS and IoT makes it difficult to form composites of services and things. For example, the streaming data collected by sensors in the IoT and the data of function-based cloud services in the IoS have totally different granularities, making it difficult to combine them. In the traditional SOA, service users can easily access and invoke Web services through standardized protocols or lightweight message transfer frameworks. However, the diversity of things and interaction styles between service users and providers in the IoT environment makes it difficult to apply the SOA approach as is. Therefore, it is necessary to consider middleware-level components for service access in IoT [32,36]. That is, we need to deal with the issues by addressing how to handle the interoperability of the services in the IoS infrastructure and things in the IoT environment.

Second, the ultra-large scale of services and things poses a huge challenge to the performance of the integrated IoS/IoT environment. Therefore, we need to deal with the issue for ensuring real-time execution of services. In a previous study, we proposed a framework of parallel service execution in the IoS infrastructure considering the policies of service providers [46]. We note that the concepts of fog computing [5] and edge computing [39] were proposed to deal with this issue in the IoT environments by handling data processing and event processing in different layers of servers. However, more factors need to be considered for improving the performance of the integrated IoS/IoT environments, including mechanisms for parallel execution of rules and handling of the massive complex event processing.

Third, the dynamics of the integrated IoS/IoT environments has two aspects: dynamic changes in available services/things, and dynamic changes in user situation. Therefore, the important issue here is that the integration framework must ensure that service composition and recommendation can accept dynamic changes in environment. Although we have conducted several studies on dynamic service selection [26] and service recommendation [10] with the Language Grid on the IoS platform, it is necessary to extend these studies into integrated IoS/IoT environments.

4 A Multiagent Perspective on Integrated IoS/IoT

4.1 Integration of IoS and IoT

For the simplicity of explaining the integration of IoS and IoT, we use the Language Grid as an example of IoS infrastructure. We developed and then operated the Language Grid as an IoS infrastructure to support intercultural collaboration for more than ten years. The Language Grid is built on general service grid server software, and consists of five parts: service manager, service supervisor, grid composer, service database, and composite service container [28]. Based on the federated service grid architecture which seamlessly connects multiple service grids [29], we also realized the federated operation of the Language Grid in several Asian countries including Japan, Thailand, Indonesia and China. As of March 2019, 226 language services are being shared on the federated Language Grid. Moreover, an extended framework for service design was proposed with the Language Grid by bridging the gap between stakeholders involved in language service infrastructures and those who develop and operate multi-language systems [25].

The key concept of IoS infrastructures like the Language Grid is to standardize the service interface for each category of resource (data, software, business process, etc.), and enable flexible service management and service composition. In IoT environments, standardization and composition of things are also regarded as important fundamentals [3]. For example, OpenIoT is one of the typical initiatives to realize standards for IoT [44], while Web of things is another proposal for composing embedded devices on IoT [11]. Moreover, a SOA-based IoT architecture has been proposed to realize flexible service composition with trust management for IoT environments [7].

There are two aspects that we should consider in the integration of IoS and IoT: development of the integrated architecture and design of real-world applications based on the integrated architecture. The remaining parts of this section will discuss these two aspects from a multiagent perspective.

4.2 The Multiagent-Based Architecture

The first aspect is how to develop the integrated architecture by addressing the complications hindering service composition and the interactions between IoS and IoT. Here we consider some typical patterns of service composition and interaction in the integrated IoS/IoT environments.

1. Information of things in the IoT is collected and aggregated by sensors, and it triggers the invocation of atomic services or composition of atomic services in the IoS platform. For example, appropriate language supporting services are invoked based on the information collected and analyzed from an eye-tracker that identifies a non-native speaker's difficulties during a multilingual conversation [6].
2. Actuators in the IoT trigger invocation of atomic services or composition of atomic services in the IoS platform. For example, the lightening of different colors of IoT LED or push of different buttons triggers the invocation of machine translation services with different input parameters (language combinations), which will be useful for multilingual support in international conferences [30].
3. Execution of atomic services or composition of atomic services in the IoS platform drives actuators or sensors on IoT. For example, whenever a composite translation service is executed by a certain user, a group of sensors like GPS and counter are driven to record the behavioral or situational data of the user together with the service invocation information, which can help improve the accuracy of situated service recommendation in the integrated IoS/IoT environments [10].

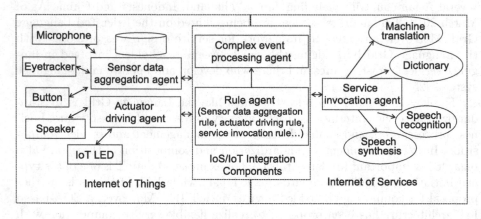

Fig. 1. Multiagent-based integration of IoS and IoT

Since there are various types of complicated interaction, we can regard the integrated IoS/IoT environments as a multiagent-based architecture as shown in Fig. 1. The interaction between IoS and IoT can be realized by complex event processing agents and rule agents that manage various rules including sensor data aggregation rules, actuator driving rules, and service invocation rules. Complex event processing agents and rule agents are key parts of the integration components. Agents in the integration components interact with sensor data aggregation agents, actuator driving agents, and service invocation agents in the IoS and IoT sides to realize service composition.

The most important feature of the multiagent-based architecture is that it should be designed to address the major issues of IoS/IoT integration described in the previous section. Traditional characteristics of multiagent systems can help deal with these issues in different ways. To deal with the heterogeneity of cloud services and IoT devices, agents in both the IoS side and the IoT side need to deal with the interoperability by interface matching and learning mechanisms. For example, sensor data aggregation agents are required to discover an unregistered sensor that has the similar interface with a known type of IoT devices. To address the challenge of ultra-large scale of services and things in the environments, the rule agents and complex event processing agents need to provide optimization mechanisms to ensure real-time processing of rules and execution of services, which can probably be realized by solving constraint optimization problems in the domain of traditional multiagent systems. To address the dynamics of the integrated IoS/IoT environments, agent adaptations need to be applied to deal with various dynamic changes, e.g. the fluctuation of available services and devices in the environments.

4.3   Multiagent Methodologies for Service Design

We discussed the possibility of using the multiagent-based approach to deal with the integrated components for IoS/IoT. However, it is also important to design the application systems to be run on the integrated IoS/IoT environments, which is the second aspect of the integration. Service design process with integrated IoS/IoT environments always involves multiple stakeholders with different incentives, and therefore multiagent methodologies can be applied.

In previous work, we studied the service design process for the IoS infrastructure [24]. To design sociotechnical systems for the real world, the iterative service design approach is always applied; it consists of four phases: the observation phase is to understand user requirements and evaluation criteria for QoS; the modeling phase is to define the service process that can best satisfy user requirements by combining available cloud services based on QoS evaluations; the implementation phase is to realize service composition by embedding composited services into application systems; the analysis phase is to evaluate the designed service by analyzing the log data and interview results based on the defined QoS evaluation criteria [22]. This iterative service design process can also be applied to the service design for integrated IoS/IoT environments.

Based on numerous experiences in service design, we adopted the multiagent approach to propose field-oriented design methodologies [15]; this allows us to deal with the service design in the field, where complex issues often arise. The service design process always starts by understanding the problems in the field and proposing services for solving those problems at an early stage. Due to the interdependency between problems and their changes over time, it is more important to develop a continuous problem solving process than to solve just current problems. In this context, multiagent methodologies were proposed for experiments on service design with multiple stakeholders, including role playing games [45], participatory simulations [21] and gaming simulations [31].

5   An Example Application of Multilingual Environment Design

As our application, we use the example of designing a multilingual environment to illustrate the integration of IoS and IoT. Figure 2 shows a scenario of multilingual conversion between an interactive agent and a user. In the scenario, a German visitor is shopping at the Nishiki Market in Kyoto, a historic Japanese marketplace; the multilingual interactive agent provides necessary support. When the visitor asks something in German, the interactive agent first selects a composite translation service to translate it into Japanese. According to the difficulty and language of the input sentences of the visitor, the service invocation agent on IoS recommends a composite translation service, which usually consists of a speech recognition service, a machine translation service, and a dictionary service of domain knowledge. Meanwhile, the sensor data aggregation agent on IoT is interacting with the rule agent and complex event processing agent by sending the event information about what the visitor is looking at. The rule agent and complex event processing agent then trigger a composite dialogue generation service by interacting with the service invocation agent. In the example shown in Fig. 2, the service invocation agent recommends a cultural-oriented dialogue generation service that maps one concept in one culture (e.g. Suguki, traditional Kyoto pickles shown in the top-right part of Fig. 2) into the close concept in the other culture (e.g. Sauerkraut, which is a well-known dish in Germany) for explanation. Similar examples of culturally-situated agent were introduced in our previous work [1,20].

The dialogue between the interactive agent and the visitor in above example seems simple, but its generation involves complicated interactions between various agents on the integrated IoS/IoT environments and service composition based on situation-aware recommendation mechanisms. To realize such high-quality multilingual environments with IoS and IoT, we must deal with two major issues: realizing key technologies of the integrated IoS/IoT architecture for service composition and designing multilingual interactive agents based on the integrated architecture.

Situated Service Composition. Service composition is one of the most important topics in the area of SOC, and this is also true in the integrated IoS/IoT environments. Traditionally, service composition is a technology that combines multiple atomic services in the IoS infrastructure to satisfy user requirements of Quality of Services (QoS). Service composition can be realized by automatically generating the service workflow through planning, constraint-based approach, QoS optimization, and user-centered approach. The key lies in how to select appropriate services to execute the service workflow since there are always numerous atomic service candidates for the same function. One of the major challenges in realizing this application is to combine various services on the integrated service platform and establishing interaction between agents across IoS and IoT. Unfortunately, existing service recommendation approaches do not fully consider the influence of situation information, such as time, location, and user relations thoroughly. Our solution is a situated QoS prediction for service recommendation that combines observed factor learning and latent factor learning. The detailed proposed mechanism is described in our previous work [10]. The situated service composition mechanism can be realized based on the multiagent integrated architecture described in Fig. 1.

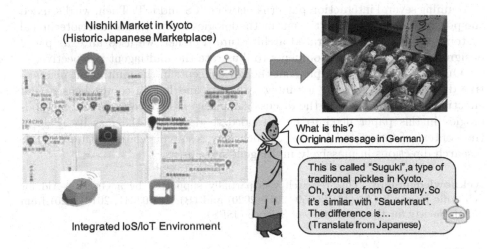

Nishiki Market in Kyoto
(Historic Japanese Marketplace)

What is this?
(Original message in German)

This is called "Suguki", a type of traditional pickles in Kyoto. Oh, you are from Germany. So it's similar with "Sauerkraut". The difference is…
(Translate from Japanese)

Integrated IoS/IoT Environment

Fig. 2. An application of multilingual environment design with IoS and IoT

Multilingual Interactive Agents. Another issue in the example application is to realize multilingual interactive agents. The interactive agents play essential roles in many fields [38]. For example, there are increasing demands in the fields of tourism and healthcare to use interactive agents because of the human resource shortage due to the aging population. In such circumstances, interactive agents are required to handle dialogues with end users in various situations. Moreover, it becomes important for interactive agents to provide multilingual support to end users. However, it is always difficult to ensure the quality of dialogues generated by the agent, especially at an early stage. Previous studies widely used Wizard of Oz (WoZ) for prototyping and evaluating dialogue-based computer systems that have not yet been realized. In our service design process, we also apply WoZ to prototype and improve the interactive agent gradually. In our proposed framework, the recommender system provides a candidate list of dialogues to the Wizard based on service composition. The Wizard then selects or creates appropriate dialogues and provides them to the interactive agent. The detailed framework of interactive agent is described in our previous studies [33]. The implementation process of the interactive agents can be regarded as a participatory social system design process, which is a multiagent approach for service design.

6   Conclusion

This paper dealt with the issues of integrating Internet of Services (IoS) and Internet of Things (IoT) for realizing Internet-based sociotechnical systems. We described the integrated IoS/IoT architecture from a multiagent perspective. First, we described the multiagent-based architecture suitable for the integration by defining several interaction patterns between IoS and IoT. Then, we discussed the possibilities of using multiagent methodologies in the design of sociotechnical systems based on the integrated architecture. Further, we used an example of designing multilingual environments to illustrate the multiagent perspective.

Our future work is to implement the key concepts in the multiagent perspective discussed in this paper for integrating IoS and IoT in comprehensive and effective manner. Moreover, the discussed multiagent architectures and methodologies in this paper need to be extended to deal with the massive scale in the context of integrated IoS/IoT, which may result in related future possible research directions in massively multiagent systems.

Acknowledgement. This research was partially supported by a Grant-in-Aid for Scientific Research (A) (17H00759, 2017–2020) and (B) (18H03341, 2018–2020) from Japan Society for the Promotion of Science (JSPS).

References

1. Abou-Khalil, V., Ishida, T., Otani, M., Flanagan, B., Ogata, H., Lin, D.: Learning culturally situated dialogue strategies to support language learners. Res. Pract. Technol. Enhanc. Learn. **13**(1), 10 (2018)
2. Al-Fuqaha, A., Guizani, M., Mohammadi, M., Aledhari, M., Ayyash, M.: Internet of Things: a survey on enabling technologies, protocols, and applications. IEEE Commun. Surv. Tutor. **17**(4), 2347–2376 (2015)
3. Bandyopadhyay, D., Sen, J.: Internet of Things: applications and challenges in technology and standardization. Wireless Pers. Commun. **58**(1), 49–69 (2011)
4. Bergenti, F., Franchi, E., Poggi, A.: Agent-based interpretations of classic network models. Comput. Math. Organ. Theory **19**(2), 105–127 (2013)
5. Bonomi, F., Milito, R., Zhu, J., Addepalli, S.: Fog computing and its role in the Internet of Things. In: Proceedings of the First Edition of the MCC Workshop on Mobile Cloud Computing, pp. 13–16. ACM (2012)
6. Cao, X., Yamashita, N., Ishida, T.: How non-native speakers perceive listening comprehension problems: implications for adaptive support technologies. In: Yoshino, T., Chen, G.-D., Zurita, G., Yuizono, T., Inoue, T., Baloian, N. (eds.) CollabTech 2016. CCIS, vol. 647, pp. 89–104. Springer, Singapore (2016). https://doi.org/10.1007/978-981-10-2618-8_8
7. Chen, R., Guo, J., Bao, F.: Trust management for SOA-based IoT and its application to service composition. IEEE Trans. Serv. Comput. **9**(3), 482–495 (2016)
8. Chopra, A.K., Singh, M.P.: From social machines to social protocols: software engineering foundations for sociotechnical systems. In: Proceedings of the 25th International Conference on World Wide Web, pp. 903–914. International World Wide Web Conferences Steering Committee (2016)

9. Da Xu, L., He, W., Li, S.: Internet of Things in industries: a survey. IEEE Trans. Industr. Inf. **10**(4), 2233–2243 (2014)
10. Dai, J., Lin, D., Ishida, T.: A two-phase method of QoS prediction for situated service recommendation. In: 2018 IEEE International Conference on Services Computing (SCC). IEEE (2018)
11. Guinard, D., Trifa, V.: Towards the web of things: web mashups for embedded devices. In: Workshop on Mashups, Enterprise Mashups and Lightweight Composition on the Web (MEM 2009), in proceedings of WWW (International World Wide Web Conferences), Madrid, Spain, vol. 15 (2009)
12. Huhns, M.N., Singh, M.P.: Service-oriented computing: key concepts and principles. IEEE Internet Comput. **9**(1), 75–81 (2005)
13. Huhns, M.N., et al.: Research directions for service-oriented multiagent systems. IEEE Internet Comput. **9**(6), 65–70 (2005)
14. Ishida, T.: The language grid: service-oriented collective intelligence for language resource interoperability. In: Ishida, T. (ed.) The Language Grid. Cognitive Technologies. Springer, Heidelberg (2011). https://doi.org/10.1007/978-3-642-21178-2_1
15. Ishida, T., et al.: Field-oriented service design: a multiagent approach. In: Maeno, T., Sawatani, Y., Hara, T. (eds.) Serviceology for Designing the Future, pp. 451–463. Springer, Tokyo (2016). https://doi.org/10.1007/978-4-431-55861-3_31
16. Ishida, T., Murakami, Y., Lin, D., Nakaguchi, T., Otani, M.: Language service infrastructure on the web: the language grid. Computer **51**(6), 72–81 (2018)
17. Issarny, V., Bouloukakis, G., Georgantas, N., Billet, B.: Revisiting service-oriented architecture for the iot: a middleware perspective. In: Sheng, Q.Z., Stroulia, E., Tata, S., Bhiri, S. (eds.) ICSOC 2016. LNCS, vol. 9936, pp. 3–17. Springer, Cham (2016). https://doi.org/10.1007/978-3-319-46295-0_1
18. Jiang, J., et al.: Understanding crowdsourcing systems from a multiagent perspective and approach. ACM Trans. Auton. Adapt. Syst. (TAAS) **13**(2), 8 (2018)
19. Jiang, Y., Jiang, J.: Diffusion in social networks: a multiagent perspective. IEEE Trans. Syst., Man, Cybern.: Syst. **45**(2), 198–213 (2015)
20. Khalil, V.A., Ishida, T., Otani, M., Lin, D.: A culturally-situated agent to support intercultural collaboration. In: Yoshino, T., Yuizono, T., Zurita, G., Vassileva, J. (eds.) CollabTech 2017. LNCS, vol. 10397, pp. 130–144. Springer, Cham (2017). https://doi.org/10.1007/978-3-319-63088-5_12
21. Lin, D., Ishida, T.: Participatory service design based on user-centered QoS. In: Proceedings of the 2013 IEEE/WIC/ACM International Joint Conferences on Web Intelligence (WI) and Intelligent Agent Technologies (IAT)-Volume 01, pp. 465–472. IEEE Computer Society (2013)
22. Lin, D., Ishida, T.: User-centered service design for multi-language knowledge communication. In: Mochimaru, M., Ueda, K., Takenaka, T. (eds.) Serviceology for Services, pp. 309–317. Springer, Tokyo (2014). https://doi.org/10.1007/978-4-431-54816-4_32
23. Lin, D., Ishida, T., Murakami, Y., Tanaka, M.: Qos analysis for service composition by human and web services. IEICE Trans. Inf. Syst. **97**(4), 762–769 (2014)
24. Lin, D., Ishida, T., Otani, M.: A value co-creation model for multi-language knowledge communication. In: Maeno, T., Sawatani, Y., Hara, T. (eds.) Serviceology for Designing the Future, pp. 435–447. Springer, Tokyo (2016). https://doi.org/10.1007/978-4-431-55861-3_30

25. Lin, D., Murakami, Y., Ishida, T.: A framework for multi-language service design with the language grid. In: Proceedings of the Eleventh International Conference on Language Resources and Evaluation (LREC 2018), 7–12 May 2018. European Language Resources Association (ELRA), Miyazaki, Japan (2018)
26. Lin, D., Shi, C., Ishida, T.: Dynamic service selection based on context-aware QoS. In: 2012 IEEE Ninth International Conference on Services Computing (SCC), pp. 641–648. IEEE (2012)
27. Murakami, Y., Lin, D., Ishida, T.: Services Computing for Language Resources. Springer, Singapore (2018). https://doi.org/10.1007/978-981-10-7793-7
28. Murakami, Y., Lin, D., Tanaka, M., Nakaguchi, T., Ishida, T.: Service grid architecture. In: Ishida, T. (ed.) The Language Grid, pp. 19–34. Springer, Heidelberg (2011). https://doi.org/10.1007/978-3-642-21178-2_2
29. Murakami, Y., Tanaka, M., Lin, D., Ishida, T.: Service grid federation architecture for heterogeneous domains. In: 2012 IEEE Ninth International Conference on Services Computing (SCC), pp. 539–546. IEEE (2012)
30. Nakaguchi, T., Otani, M., Takasaki, T., Ishida, T.: Combining human inputters and language services to provide multi-language support system for international symposiums. In: Proceedings of the Third International Workshop on Worldwide Language Service Infrastructure and Second Workshop on Open Infrastructures and Analysis Frameworks for Human Language Technologies (WLSI/OIAF4HLT2016), pp. 28–35 (2016)
31. Nakajima, Y., Otsuka, R., Hishiyama, R., Nakaguchi, T., Oda, N.: Gaming for language services. In: Murakami, Y., Lin, D., Ishida, T. (eds.) Services Computing for Language Resources. CT, pp. 193–208. Springer, Singapore (2018). https://doi.org/10.1007/978-981-10-7793-7_12
32. Ngu, A.H., Gutierrez, M., Metsis, V., Nepal, S., Sheng, Q.Z.: IoT middleware: a survey on issues and enabling technologies. IEEE Internet Things J. 4(1), 1–20 (2017)
33. Okuno, R., Lin, D., Ishida, T., Otani, M.: Realizing multilingual interactive agents through wizard of Oz. In: 2017 International Conference on Culture and Computing (Culture and Computing), pp. 155–156. IEEE (2017)
34. Papazoglou, M.P., Traverso, P., Dustdar, S., Leymann, F.: Service-oriented computing: state of the art and research challenges. Computer 40(11), 38–45 (2007)
35. Papazoglou, M.P.: Service-oriented computing: concepts, characteristics and directions. In: 2003 Proceedings of the Fourth International Conference on Web Information Systems Engineering, WISE 2003, pp. 3–12. IEEE (2003)
36. Razzaque, M.A., Milojevic-Jevric, M., Palade, A., Clarke, S.: Middleware for internet of things: a survey. IEEE Internet Things J. 3(1), 70–95 (2016)
37. Schroth, C., Janner, T.: Web 2.0 and SOA: converging concepts enabling the internet of services. IT Prof. 9(3), 36–41 (2007)
38. Shi, C., Ishida, T., Lin, D.: Translation agent: a new metaphor for machine translation. New Gener. Comput. 32(2), 163–186 (2014)
39. Shi, W., Cao, J., Zhang, Q., Li, Y., Xu, L.: Edge computing: vision and challenges. IEEE Internet Things J. 3(5), 637–646 (2016)
40. Singh, M.P.: Norms as a basis for governing sociotechnical systems. ACM Trans. Intell. Syst. Technol. (TIST) 5(1), 21 (2013)
41. Singh, M.P., Chopra, A.K.: The internet of things and multiagent systems: decentralized intelligence in distributed computing. In: 2017 IEEE 37th International Conference on Distributed Computing Systems (ICDCS), pp. 1738–1747. IEEE (2017)

42. Singh, M.P., Chopra, A.K., Desai, N.: Commitment-based service-oriented architecture. Computer **42**(11), 72–79 (2009)
43. Singh, M.P., Huhns, M.N.: Service-Oriented Computing: Semantics, Processes, Agents. Wiley, Chichester (2005)
44. Soldatos, J., et al.: OpenIoT: open source Internet-of-Things in the cloud. In: Podnar Žarko, I., Pripužić, K., Serrano, M. (eds.) Interoperability and Open-Source Solutions for the Internet of Things. LNCS, vol. 9001, pp. 13–25. Springer, Cham (2015). https://doi.org/10.1007/978-3-319-16546-2_3
45. Torii, D., Ishida, T., Bousquet, F.: Modeling agents and interactions in agricultural economics. In: Proceedings of the Fifth International Joint Conference on Autonomous Agents and Multiagent Systems, pp. 81–88. ACM (2006)
46. Trang, M.X., Murakami, Y., Ishida, T.: Policy-aware service composition: predicting parallel execution performance of composite services. IEEE Trans. Serv. Comput. **11**(4), 602–615 (2018). https://doi.org/10.1109/TSC.2015.2467330
47. Weiss, G.: Multiagent Systems: A Modern Approach to Distributed Artificial Intelligence. MIT press, Cambridge (1999)
48. Wooldridge, M.: An Introduction to Multiagent Systems. Wiley, New York (2009)
49. Zambonelli, F., Jennings, N.R., Wooldridge, M.: Developing multiagent systems: the Gaia methodology. ACM Trans. Softw. Eng. Methodol. (TOSEM) **12**(3), 317–370 (2003)
50. Zeng, L., Benatallah, B., Ngu, A.H., Dumas, M., Kalagnanam, J., Chang, H.: Qos-aware middleware for web services composition. IEEE Trans. Softw. Eng. **30**(5), 311–327 (2004)

Architectures for Massively Multi-agent Systems

Two-Layer Architecture for Distributed Massively Multi-agent Systems

Yohei Murakami[1(✉)], Takao Nakaguchi[2], Donghui Lin[3], and Toru Ishida[3]

[1] Faculty of Information Science and Engineering, Ritsumeikan University,
1-1-1 Noji-Higashi, Shiga 525-8577, Japan
`yohei@fc.ritsumei.ac.jp`
[2] The Kyoto College of Graduate Studies for Informatics,
10-5 Nishi-Kujo Teranomae-Machi, Kyoto 601-8407, Japan
`ta_nakaguchi@kcg.edu`
[3] Department of Social Informatics, Kyoto University, Yoshida-Honmachi,
Kyoto 606-8501, Japan
`{lindh,ishida}@i.kyoto-u.ac.jp`

Abstract. Existing massively multi-agent systems are aimed at handling tens of thousands of agents on a single server or a computer cluster. To this end, the agents are implemented as a data structure on the server to run at high speed. However, in future IoS/IoT environments, it will be necessary to deploy agents to distributed servers. Therefore, we propose a two-layered architecture consisting of macro-agents and micro-agents: the former controls the distributed environment and the latter solves the problem cooperatively. The macro-agents pre-installed on servers form a self-organized network by communicating with neighbor macro-agents. On the other hand, micro-agents are implemented as data structures on the server and solve problems under control of the macro-agents. An example scenario is presented to illustrate how to apply the proposed architecture to driving assistance with environment-embedded sensors.

Keywords: Massively multi-agent systems · Distributed systems

1 Introduction

The development of IoT (Internet of Things) requires large-scale multi-agent systems (Massively Multi-Agent Systems) that can handle several million agents deployed on distributed devices such as sensors in a real environment. However, existing massively multi-agent systems focus on parallel processing, not large-scale distributed processing, because all agents were assumed to be deployed on a single server.

The agent server named Caribbean implemented an agent swap in/out technology to control memory and handle threads for large numbers of agents [11,12]. Caribbean represents agents as a data structure. The agent swap technology unloads some agents and loads others into memory to implement a huge number of agents at high speed given that runtime processes will most likely not

© Springer Nature Switzerland AG 2019
D. Lin et al. (Eds.): MMAS 2018, LNAI 11422, pp. 53–65, 2019.
https://doi.org/10.1007/978-3-030-20937-7_4

have enough memory to load all agents. CyberOrgs is a layered architecture for distributed multi-agent systems [2–4]. This focuses on resource management for agents that share distributed resources, but it lacks the perspective of open network, where agents will often join and leave. However, it is required to deploy massive numbers of agents on tens of thousands of networked servers in the future open IoT environment where nodes will dynamically change.

In designing such a large-scale open distributed system, it is impossible to know available agents beforehand. To solve this problem, we need to separate implementation of the application logic (hereafter called *scenarios*) from meta control that discovers available agents, assigns scenarios to them, and coordinates the communication between them.

Therefore, this paper proposes a two-layered architecture for multi-agent systems; it combines *micro-agents* that concentrate on problem-solving with *macro-agents* that manage micro agents. The macro-agents are pre-installed on each server and network with other macro-agents in a self-organized way. On the other hand, the micro-agents are implemented as data structures on the servers and solve application-specific problems following the scenarios assigned under macro-agents' control. This system is named MMAS2L (Massively Multi-Agent System with 2 Layers).

To allow macro-agents to coordinate interaction between micro-agents, we have addressed the following issues.

Design two-layer architecture
In an open system where agents freely join and leave, it is necessary to separate scenario implementation from scenario assignment to agents and to dynamically bind scenarios to agents according to the execution environment available. To this end, we need to design a two-layered multi-agent system architecture consisting of two types of agents: the ones that solve application-specific problems, and the others that discover the former and assign scenarios to them.

Language specification for meta scenarios
To split meta-level control among problem-solving agents and the assignment of application-specific scenarios, we need a way to describe a meta-scenario for meta-level agents. Therefore, we must create a language suitable for describing meta scenarios.

This paper starts by explaining the two-layer multi-agent system architecture in Sect. 2 and then defines a language for describing meta scenarios in Sect. 3. Lastly, we introduce an example of meta scenarios as applied to connected vehicles in Sect. 4.

2   Two-Layer Architecture

This section outlines a two-layer multi-agent system architecture consisting of micro-agents executing scenarios and macro-agents executing meta-scenarios.

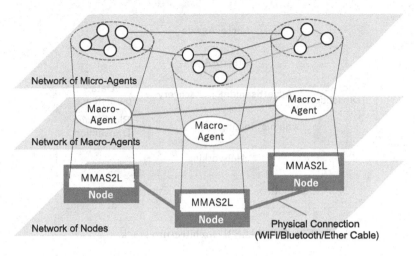

Fig. 1. Massively multi-agent system with 2 layers.

2.1   Overlay Networks

To develop a multi-agent system for an open distributed environment, an overlay network independent of physical networks is required so that the micro-agents become independent of network configuration. To this end, we will introduce macro-agents that organize an overlay network into a multi-agent system. The macro-agents discover other macro-agents by using the physical network and organize a virtual network of macro-agents. The macro-agents also construct an overlay network for micro-agents that allows shared execution of an application scenario and supports communications between micro-agents. As shown in Fig. 1, MMAS2L forms a two-layer overlay network of macro-agents and micro-agents on a physical network.

2.2   Overall Architecture

Figure 2 illustrates the MMAS2L architecture stack. The bottom layer holds the physical links such as Bluetooth and ethernet/WiFi. The second layer organizes a network of nodes pre-installed with macro-agents. This layer is responsible for detecting macro-agents' participation and withdrawal. The third layer is dynamic routing. This layer routes messages in the dynamically-organized network. The fourth layer offers synchronous or asynchronous communication, advertisements like broadcasting, and discovery. By using those functionalities, macro-agents find available micro-agents that can execute a given scenario, and create an overlay network consisting of those micro-agents. This overlay network allows micro-agents to communicate with each other simply by using just micro-agent ID. Furthermore, the third and fourth layer provides blockchain-based data management for data persistence.

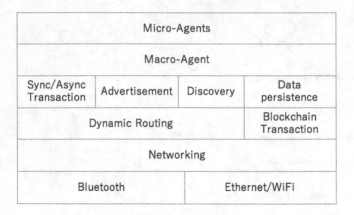

Micro-Agents			
Macro-Agent			
Sync/Async Transaction	Advertisement	Discovery	Data persistence
Dynamic Routing			Blockchain Transaction
Networking			
Bluetooth		Ethernet/WiFi	

Fig. 2. MMAS2L architecture stack.

2.3   Macro Agents

Macro-agents act autonomously according to a given meta scenario while remaining on their pre-installed server. They first access a network predefined in their meta scenario and search for other macro-agents to organize a network of macro-agents. We assume the existence of several search modes. For example, they can form a network of geographically-adjacent macro-agents by using an ad-hoc network. Also, it is possible to prevent the network from expanding larger than necessary by linking to only other macro-agents that control micro-agents interacting with their micro-agents. Moreover, they can flexibly adjust the network according to node changes by sensing macro-agents' participation and withdrawal to/from the network. In the dynamically-organized network, macro-agents need to discover available micro-agents who can conduct a given scenario in order to construct an overlay network of micro-agents. Therefore, they use a contract net protocol to find suitable micro-agents within the network of macro-agents. After the network of macro-agents is established, they control communications between massive micro-agents distributed across a huge number of servers and migrate micro-agents depending on load status and network traffic of each server.

2.4   Micro Agents

Micro-agents solve an application-specific problem in accordance with a given scenario. The scenario allows the micro-agents to communicate with each other by their ID assigned by the overlay network provided by their macro-agents because the overlay network separates the scenario description from the physical distributed environment. Furthermore, the overlay network shares events among micro-agents that implement the same scenarios so that the micro-agents can synchronously process their scenarios in an event-driven manner.

3   Meta Scenario

This section explains a language suitable for meta scenarios that demand the control of massively-distributed multi-agent systems.

3.1   Scenario Description Language Q

To deploy a large number of agents across several tens of thousands of networked servers like IoT, it is necessary to separate application logic from meta-control that discovers available agents, assigns a scenario to them, and coordinates communication between them.

This paper employs the scenario description language Q to describe a scenario of application logic. Q is a language created to describe interactions between an agent and the environment including other agents [1]. This allows application developers to define agent behavior using their defined vocabularies suitable to their domain because Q does not focus on the internal mechanism of the agents. Q has already been used to describe agent behavior in multi-agent simulations and an evacuation-guidance system [7,8].

In Q, a scenario is represented as an extended finite state machine. The scenario consists of cues that require the agent to sense an event triggering a state transition and actions that require the agent to affect its environment. The main language functionalities of Q are explained below.

Cue and Action

An event that triggers interaction is called a cue. requireagents to observe their environment. No cue is permitted to have any side effect. Cues wait for the event specified until the observation is completed successfully. Once a cue has been successfully performed, it returns #t. Cues are defined by defcue. Each cue name begins with ?, such as ?hear and ?see.

Comparable to cues, actions are used to request agents to change their environment. Two types of actions are prepared. One type is asynchronous action, which can be executed independently of other actions; following actions do not have to wait for completion of asynchronous actions. The other type, synchronous actions, cannot be executed in parallel with other actions, and the following actions have to wait for their completion.

Action is defined by defaction. Once an action has been successfully performed, it returns #t. Each synchronous action name begins with !, and asynchronous action names with !!. If a particular action needs to have both properties, we define both synchronous and asynchronous versions of the action (i.e. !walk and !!walk).

Unlike functions in programming languages, the semantics of cues and actions are not defined by Q. Since cues and actions are executed differently by different agents, their semantics fully depend on the agent's implementation.

Guarded Command/Scenario

A guarded command is used to wait for several cues simultaneously. When any of the cues is observed, the subsequent forms are executed. A scenario is used for describing state transitions, and is defined by defscenario. Each state is defined as a guarded command, but can also include conditions in addition to cues. Scenarios can be called from other scenarios or functions.

For state transition, (go state) is used in forms following cues. In the case that no state transition happens during the execution of forms, the scenario terminates. A scenario returns the value of its last form.

Program 1. Definition of scenario

```
1 (defscenario chat
2    (&pattern ($agent #f))
3    (greeting
4       ((?hear :from $agent :word "Hello")
5        (!speak :to $agent :sentence "Hello")
6        (go greeting))
7       ((?hear :from $agent :word "Bye")
8        (!speak :to $agent :sentence "Bye"))))
```

Take the example of a chat scenario consisting of one state; "greeting." In the "greeting" state, which is the initial state, the agent waits to hear "Hello" or "Bye" from someone. If the agent hears "Hello," it replies "Hello." If the agent hears "Bye," it replies "Bye." In both of cases, the agent returns to "greeting" state to wait for hearing "Hello" or "Bye."

Agent

An agent is generated by defining it with defagent. Two keyword arguments are required to define an agent. One, scenario, is to assign a specific scenario to the agent, and the other, population, is to specify the number of agents to be generated for the same scenario. Note that these keyword arguments are optional. If keyword argument scenario is omitted, it is necessary to explicitly describe scenario invocations. If keyword argument population is omitted, the number of agents is set to one.

Program 2. Definition of agents

```
1 (defagent participants
2    :scenario chat
3    :population 10)
```

The above example defines agent "participants" to execute scenario "chat." A unique ID is assigned to each agent. This ID can be acquired by evaluating each agent's name. If population is more than two, the list of IDs is bound to the name of agents.

Table 1. Vocabulary for meta-scenario.

Type	Vocabulary	Explanation
Definition	`defmetascenario`	Define a meta-scenario
	`defmacroagent`	Define a macro-agent
	`defnetwork`	Define a physical network used to construct a network of macro-agents
Network control	`!useNetwork`	Use the network defined by `defnetwork` to construct a macro-agent network
	`!getNetwork`	Get the used network information
	`!setNetwork`	Update the used network information
	`?join`	Sense a macro-agent joining the used network
	`?leave`	Sense a macro-agent leaving the used network
Scenario execution	`!announce`	Announce a scenario to macro-agents in the used network
	`!bid`	Bid for the announced scenario
	`?receiveAnnouncement`	Receive an announcement
	`?receiveBid`	Receive a bid
	`!bind`	Bind a scenario to a micro-agent
	`!unbind`	Unbind a scenario from a micro-agent
	`?finish`	Sense micro-agent completion of a scenario
	`!migrate`	Migrate a micro-agent to another macro-agent

3.2 Extension of Q for Meta-scenario

The current version of Q does not support an open distributed environment where agents can freely join and leave because it assumes scenarios are to be assigned to agents created beforehand. We need a meta scenario to control scenario execution such as dynamically creating agents according to the current environment and flexibly assigning scenarios to newly created agents to organize a multi-agent system.

In this paper, we employ an extended finite state machine to describe a meta scenario, which is used to control multi-agent simulations [13]. Therefore, we use the existing cues, actions, and guarded commands provided by Q to define cues and actions for describing a meta scenario. Table 1 summarizes the defined cues and actions.

The vocabularies are classified into three types: definition, network control, and scenario execution management. The first defines a physical network for distributed processing as well as the definitions of a meta scenario and macro-agents. Macro-agents need to search for other macro-agents and establish a network with them to enable collaboration among micro-agents. The formed network depends on the search range permitted by the physical network. To define the search range of the physical network for exploration, we use `defnetwork`. For instance, when we use a static network, the network is defined as a list of IP addresses of servers running macro agents. On the other hand, when we organize geographically adjacent macro-agents, the network is defined by the number of hops in an ad-hoc network. That is, one hop means only macro-agents within the same WiFi cell compose a network.

The second one defines cues and actions for controlling a network of macro-agents. `!useNetwork` is used to organize a network of macro-agents on the physical network defined by `defnetwork`. Once the network is established, the network must adapt to dynamic node changes. Therefore, `?join` and `?leave` are used to sense macro-agents' participation and withdrawal to/from the network. To reconfigure the network according to the observed participation and withdrawal, we define `!getNetwork` to get the current setting values and `!setNetwork` to update the values. In the case of switching the network, `!useNetwork` is used again to replace it with the new network defined by `defnetwork`.

The third one defines cues and actions for organizing a team of micro-agents to solve an application-specific problem. A macro-agent firstly announces a scenario to other macro-agents within the network to call for collaboration. Upon receiving the announcement, the macro-agents who host micro-agents that can conduct the scenario bid for the scenario. The announcing macro-agent chooses appropriate micro-agents from the bids and assigns the scenario to them. To implement this contract net protocol, we define two actions and two cues: `!announceTask`, `!bid`, `?receiveAnnouncement`, and `?receiveBid`. Furthermore, we also bind/unbind a scenario to/from a micro-agent by using `!bind` and `!unbind`, and wait for the micro-agent to finish the scenario by using `?finish`. If the micro-agent must be moved to another macro-agent due to resource shortages or network traffic, `!migrate` is used.

3.3 Example of Meta-scenario

This section presents an example of meta-scenario that switches micro-agents executing a scenario according to a dynamic environment. Figure 3 illustrates the

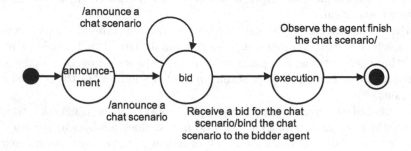

Fig. 3. State transition diagram of a typical meta-scenario.

Program 3. Example of meta-scenario

```
1 (defnetwork neighbours
2    :type "adhoc"
3    :hop 1)
4
5 (defmetascenario casual-chat
6    (&pattern ($micro #f)
7     &pattern ($macro #f))
8    (announcement
9        (#t
10           (!useNetwork :name neighbours)
11           (!announce :scenario 'chat :to neighbours)
12           (go bid)))
13   (bid
14       ((?receiveBid :agent $micro :scenario 'chat :from $macro)
15        (!bind :scenario 'chat :to $micro)
16        (go execution))
17       (otherwise
18        (!announce :scenario 'chat :to neighbours)))
19   (execution
20       ((?finish :scenario 'chat :agent $micro))))
```

example as a state transition diagram. A circle and an arrow represent a state and a state transition, respectively. Also, cues triggering a state transition and actions with the transition are labeled on the arrow by the form of (cue/action).

The example meta-scenario consists of three states: announcement of scenario, bid processing, and execution of scenario. In the first state, a macro-agent advertises for available micro-agents that can conduct the "chat" scenario in a network of macro-agents. In the bidding state, the macro-agent waits for other macro-agents to bid for the scenario. If the macro-agent receives a bid, it assigns the scenario to the bidding micro-agent and moves to the execution state. Otherwise, the macro-agent announces it again. In the execution state, when the macro-agent senses the micro-agent finish the scenario, it completes the meta-scenario.

Program 3 describes the meta-scenario by using cues and actions defined in Table 1. In this example, the macro-agent explores its WiFi network to discover available micro-agents that can conduct the "chat" scenario because this example defines a network as a one-hop ad-hoc network.

4 Application

This section introduces an application of MMAS2L to IoT. This application is a driving assistance system using environment-embedded sensors to detect events at blind spots.

4.1 Driving Control Using Environment-Embedded Sensors

The connected vehicles are assumed to have various on-board sensors such as cameras and radar for sensing, however, they are not sufficient to detect events

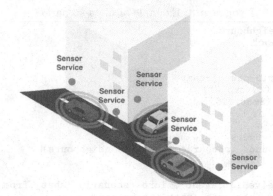

Fig. 4. Driving assistant system to detect events at blind spots.

at blind spots. By using sensors embedded in the environment as shown in Fig. 4, we can address such problems and enhance the reliability and accuracy of event detection [5].

To implement this application with MMAS2L, we pre-install macro-agents in networked edge servers and deploy micro-agents on sensors connected to the edge servers. Also, a macro-agent is set in each vehicle to host a vehicle micro-agent. Figure 5 shows how the multi-agent system is dynamically self-organized in each layer of macro-agents and micro-agents as a vehicle moves. The meta-scenario of this application is presented as a state transition diagram in Fig. 6.

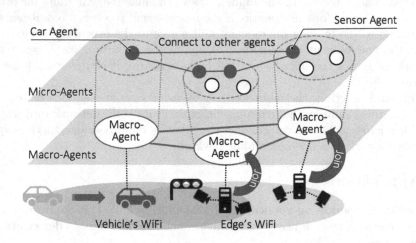

Fig. 5. Multi-agent system for driving assistance.

In this meta-scenario, a vehicle macro-agent organizes a network of macro-agents using a two-hop ad-hoc network. The macro-agent announces "notify"

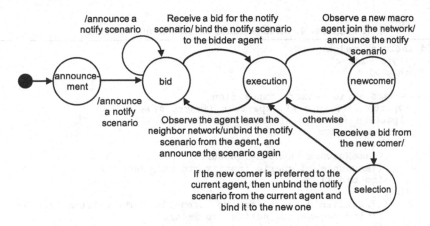

Fig. 6. State transition diagram of the meta-scenario for vehicle macro-agent.

scenario to the other macro-agents within the network. Macro-agents hosting available sensor micro-agents that can execute the "notify" scenario can bid for the scenario. When the vehicle macro-agent receives a bid, it binds the "notify" scenario to the sensor micro-agent.

The macro-agent hosting the sensor micro-agent may leave the network as the vehicle moves. In this case, the vehicle macro-agent unbinds the scenario from the sensor micro-agent and announces the "notify" scenario to other macro-agents within the network again. On the other hand, a new macro-agent may join the network as the vehicle moves. To find a more appropriate or preferable sensor micro-agent, the macro-agent also announces the scenario whenever the vehicle macro-agent senses a new macro-agent participating in the network. If the vehicle macro-agent receives a bid from a more preferable sensor micro-agent, it rebinds the "notify" scenario to the new sensor micro-agent. By continuously discovering a new or alternative micro-agents, this multi-agent system can provide a driving assistance service that follows the moving car. Program 4 describes the meta-scenario by using cues and actions defined in Table 1.

5   Conclusion

In this paper, we proposed MMAS2L, a two-layer architecture consisting of micro-agents and macro-agents to develop large-scale distributed multi-agent systems in an open environment. The micro-agents solve an application-specific problem following a given scenario, while the macro-agents coordinate with other macro-agents to construct an overlay-network among micro-agents. The purpose of the macro-agents is to separate application logic from the physical network. To this end, the macro-agents route messages among micro-agents and migrate micro-agents according to resource availability and network traffic. Moreover, we extended the existing scenario description language Q to describe meta-scenarios that control scenario execution by micro-agents. To describe the meta-scenario

Program 4. Meta-scenario for vehicle macro-agent.

```
 1 (defnetwork neighbours
 2    :type "adhoc"
 3    :hop 2)
 4
 5 (defmetascenario sensor-composition
 6    (&pattern ($micro #f) &pattern ($macro #f)
 7     &pattern ($nmicro #f) &pattern ($nmacro #f))
 8    (announcement
 9       (#t
10         (!useNetwork :name neighbours)
11         (!announce :scenario 'notify :to neighbours)
12         (go bid)))
13    (bid
14       ((?receiveBid :agent $micro :scenario 'notify :from $macro)
15         (!bind :scenario 'notify :to $micro)
16         (go execution))
17       (otherwise
18         (!announce :scenario 'notify :to neighbours)
19         (go bid)))
20    (execution
21       ((?leave :agent $macro :from neighbours)
22         (!unbind :scenario 'notify :from $micro)
23         (!announce :scenario 'notify :to neighbours)
24         (set! $macro #f)
25         (set! $micro #f)
26         (go bid))
27       ((?join :agent $nmacro :to neighbours)
28         (!announce :scenario 'notify :to neighbours)
29         (set! $nmicro #f)
30         (set! $nmacro #f)
31         (go newcomer)))
32    (newcomer
33       ((?receiveBid :agent $nmicro :scenario 'notify :from $nmacro)
34         (go selection))
35       (otherwise
36         (go execution)))
37    (selection
38       ((prefer? $nmicro $micro)
39         (!unbind :scenario 'notify :from $micro)
40         (!bind :scenario 'notify :to $nmicro)
41         (set! $micro $nmicro)
42         (set! $macro $nmacro)
43         (go execution))
44       (otherwise
45         (go execution)))))
```

usage, an application for connected-vehicles was presented. MMAS2L is applicable to the Internet as well as geographically restricted networks. In the future, we plan to use MMAS2L to construct a distributed crowdsourcing system for creating low-resourced language resources. In this system, an editor micro-agent discovers worker micro-agents that can understand target languages and makes a group to create a bilingual dictionary or parallel corpus on demand [6,9,10].

Acknowledgements. This research was partially supported by a Grant-in-Aid for Scientific Research (A) (17H00759, 2017–2020), a Grant-in-Aid for Scientific Research (B) (18H03341, 2018-2020), and a Grant-in-Aid for Young Scientists (A) (17H04706, 2017–2020) from Japan Society for the Promotion of Science (JSPS).

References

1. Ishida, T.: Q: a scenario description language for interactive agents. IEEE Comput. **35**(11), 42–47 (2002)
2. Jamali, N., Ren, S.: A layered architecture for real-time distributed multi-agent systems. ACM SIGSOFT Softw. Eng. Notes **30**(4), 1–8 (2005)
3. Jamali, N., Zhao, X.: Hierarchical resource usage coordination for large-scale multi-agent systems. In: Ishida, T., Gasser, L., Nakashima, H. (eds.) MMAS 2004. LNCS (LNAI), vol. 3446, pp. 40–54. Springer, Heidelberg (2005). https://doi.org/10.1007/11512073_4
4. Jamali, N., Zhao, X.: A scalable approach to multi-agent resource acquisition and control. In: 4th International Joint Conference on Autonomous Agents and Multiagent Systems (AAMAS 2005), Utrecht, The Netherlands, 25–29 July 2005, pp. 868–875 (2005)
5. Koyama, J., Murakami, Y., Lin, D.: Situated sensor composition for event-based system. In: 2017 IEEE International Conference on Services Computing, SCC 2017, Honolulu, HI, USA, 25–30 June 2017, pp. 212–219 (2017). https://doi.org/10.1109/SCC.2017.34
6. Murakami, Y.: Indonesia language sphere: an ecosystem for dictionary development for low-resource languages. J. Phys. Conf. Ser. (2019)
7. Murakami, Y., Ishida, T., Kawasoe, T., Hishiyama, R.: Scenario description for multi-agent simulation. In: The Second International Joint Conference on Autonomous Agents & Multiagent Systems, AAMAS 2003, Melbourne, Victoria, Australia, 14–18 July 2003, Proceedings, pp. 369–376 (2003)
8. Nakajima, Y., Shiina, H., Yamane, S., Yamaki, H., Ishida, T.: Caribbean/Q: a massively multi-agent platform with scenario description language. In: 2006 International Conference on Semantics, Knowledge and Grid (SKG 2006), Guilin, China, 1–3 November 2006, p. 26 (2006)
9. Nasution, A.H., Murakami, Y., Ishida, T.: Plan optimization for creating bilingual dictionaries of low-resource languages. In: 2017 International Conference on Culture and Computing, Culture and Computing 2017, Kyoto, Japan, 10–12 September 2017, pp. 35–41 (2017)
10. Nasution, A.H., Murakami, Y., Ishida, T.: A generalized constraint approach to bilingual dictionary induction for low-resource language families. ACM Trans. Asian Low-Resource Lang. Inf. Process. **17**(2), 9:1–9:29 (2018)
11. Yamamoto, G.: Agent server technology for managing millions of agents. In: Ishida, T., Gasser, L., Nakashima, H. (eds.) MMAS 2004. LNCS (LNAI), vol. 3446, pp. 1–12. Springer, Heidelberg (2005). https://doi.org/10.1007/11512073_1
12. Yamamoto, G., Tai, H., Mizuta, H.: A platform for massive agent-based simulation and its evaluation. In: Jamali, N., Scerri, P., Sugawara, T. (eds.) AAMAS 2007. LNCS (LNAI), vol. 5043, pp. 1–12. Springer, Heidelberg (2008). https://doi.org/10.1007/978-3-540-85449-4_1
13. Yamane, S., Ishida, T.: Meta-level control architecture for massively multiagent simulations. In: Proceedings of the Winter Simulation Conference, WSC 2006, Monterey, California, USA, 3–6 December 2006, pp. 889–896 (2006)

Multi-agent Social Simulation for Social Service Design

Itsuki Noda(✉)

The National Institute of Advanced Industrial Science and Technology (AIST),
Tsukuba, Japan
i.noda@aist.go.jp

Abstract. Multi-agent social simulation (MASS) can be a powerful tool
for designing social systems and services. Due to increases in computational power and progress in the social big data field, we can now apply
MASS to real social systems, such as urban traffic and disaster response
scenarios. Here, we demonstrate several MASS applications and discuss
future possibilities and issues in this emerging domain.

Keywords: Multi-agent social simulation ·
Computational social science · Multi-agent systems ·
High-performance computing

1 Introduction

Computational social science is becoming a practical and useful tool for analyzing, evaluating, and designing social systems. In particular, multi-agent social
simulation (MASS) can be utilized to predict social phenomena in rare or novel
situations such as disasters and future social scenarios. In addition, recent IT
developments, such as big data and high performance computing (HPC), have
brought computational social science to a point where it can be applied at a
practical engineering level.

Exhaustive simulation is one of the most fundamental elements of MASS
applications. The most significant weakness of MASS is the uncertainty of its
simulation models. Most MASS must include human behaviors as key components of the simulation, but even cutting-edge models are not yet sufficiently
accurate to explain human behavior precisely. Consequently, we cannot simply
construct a single simulation and hope to predict future social phenomena accu-
rately. Exhaustive simulation enables us to deal with this weakness and obtain
a useful information from the simulation results.

In this article, I describe several MASS applications in the pedestrian and
traffic domains, and show how exhaustive MASS can be utilized in practice in
the social service field.

D. Lin et al. (Eds.): MMAS 2018, LNAI 11422, pp. 66–80, 2019.
https://doi.org/10.1007/978-3-030-20937-7_5

2   Pedestrian Simulations

The main aim of pedestrian simulations is to predict the behavior of large crowds that are walking in a certain area or along a given road network, and to evaluate methods of managing such crowds. They are often used to support the evaluation of evacuation plans for disaster situations or to design passageway layouts and management strategies for large events. In these scenarios, each agent sets the speed and direction in which it walks based on its own goal, tendencies/preferences, knowledge, and surroundings. In the above applications, the walking agents are also crowded together such that their behavior affects that of other agent. In this section, I describe two applications of MASS to evacuation scenarios.

Multi-agent evacuation simulations will become an important tool for guiding disasters management plans. Relatively few disasters or accidents have required large-scale evacuations; therefore, it is difficult to obtain sufficiently large dataset about such disasters to predict crowd behavior via big data analysis. MASS is, therefore, an indispensable tool for designing evacuation plans.

However, when we conducting pedestrian simulations for evacuation scenarios, we need to assess the simulation results very carefully. A straight-forward way to apply evacuation simulations is to seek an *optimal* evacuation plan/guidance for the given situation, but, this is unfeasible with current technology for two reasons. The first issue is current human behavior models are not sufficiently accurate. Unlike in physics, we do not have precise human behavior models; therefore, we cannot construct simulations that will take the given circumstances and predict future phenomena with absolute accuracy. The second issue is typically lack of the information to fully determine the simulation conditions in disaster situations. Even if Internet of things (IoT) devices are deployed widely across the town, there is still no guarantee we will obtain sufficient information about the area, especially under disaster conditions, to run precise simulations.

In our projects, we have overcome these issues by following two rules. The first is to run a large number of simulations under various conditions exhausting all possible scenarios and repeating the process until we have obtained accurate statistics illustrating the properties of each evacuation plan. The second rule is not to use simulation results to answer evacuation plan optimization requests directly. Instead, we aim to support the directors/leaders in making disaster response decisions by showing them the characteristics of particular disaster situations and the phenomena that are likely to occur during evacuation.

2.1   Efficiency/Complexity Trade-Off Analysis for Evacuation Guidance

In evacuation planning, we must generally strike a balance between evacuation time and the simplicity of the evacuation guidance. If we were to focus purely on minimizing the evacuation time, it would be best to apply a mathematical optimization technique such as maximum network-flow [3]. However, we also need to guide large numbers of people, including many who are not acquainted with the area, such as visitors; therefore, the guidance must also be simple enough to understand and follow easily.

To investigate the relationship between these two objectives, we applied a non-dominated sorting genetic algorithm (NSGA-II) [1], which is a genetic algorithm (GA) for multiple objective optimization.

Here, the first objective function is the total evacuation time, estimated by simulating the pedestrian behavior under a given guidance plan.

For the second objective function, which measured the evacuation plan's simplicity, we introduced "entropy" of the plan, as follows (Fig. 1). Suppose two connecting zones, z_i and z_j in the target area have populations of n_i and n_j, respectively. If the plan's guidance for both zones sends pedestrians to the same intermediate and final points, then the entropy of this zone pair is zero. Otherwise, the entropy of is calculated as:

$$H(z_i, z_j) = -(n_i/(n_i + n_j)) \log(n_i/(n_i + n_j)) - (n_j/(n_i + n_j)) \log(n_j/(n_i + n_j)).$$

Finally, we use total entropy $H = \sum_{z_i, z_j} H(z_i, z_j)$ as a measure of the plan's complexity (opposite value of its simplicity).

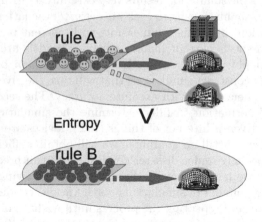

Fig. 1. Rule entropy

To simulate various evacuation scenarios, we employed CrowdWalk [15,16]. CrowdWalk is a pedestrian simulator that limits each person to move one dimensionally along a given road network. The road network is composed of nodes and links, and CrowdWalk can rapidly simulate the motion of large number of pedestrians.

We used a road map of Nishiyodogawa-ku, consisting of 7,624 nodes (intersections) and 10,707 road links (Fig. 2). This area has 86 official disaster refuges and a population of 54,909, distributed across 146 smaller zones. We assumed that each person in a given zone followed the same guidance rule, which asked them to go to a particular destination with one intermediate point both marked

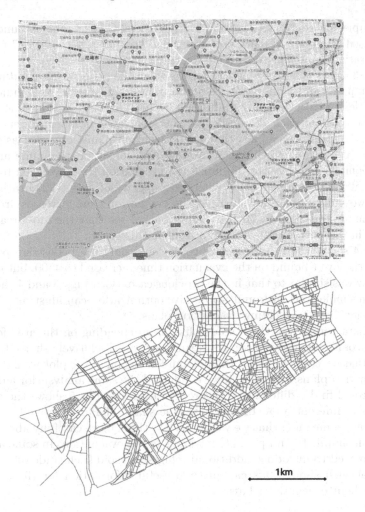

Fig. 2. Nishiyodogawa-ku area (top) and road map (bottom) used for the pedestrian simulation

on a map. The destinations and intermediate points were selected from the 86 official refuges and a set of 533 major intersections, respectively.

To apply NSGA-II to this guidance plan, we utilized OACIS (see Sect. 4) to manage the large number of runs required. The search space of this problem is huge ($R^{73} \times 533^{146} \times 86^{146}$) and NSGA-II requires a large number of populations (about 100–1,000) of individuals in GA; therefore, we needed to run the simulator many times to achieve optimal results. For this experiment, we ran the optimization process with 100 populations over 500 generations. Also, we ran 10 simulations for one guidance plan to calculate average evacuation time. In total, we ran 500,000 simulations.

We implemented NSGA-II using Ruby API of OACIS. For the underlying GA, we used "simulated binary crossover" and "polynomial mutation" to create new generations, and Paleto ranking for the selection.

Figure 3 shows the experimental results when the pedestrians could use both pedestrian paths and main roads. Here, horizontal and vertical axes indicate the plan complexity (total entropy multiplied by 100), and evacuation time, respectively. The color of each dot indicates the associated number of generations. From these results, we can see that the evacuation plans improved as the GA progressed, converging to limits of around 3000 for evacuation time and 2100 for plan complexity. Here, to minimize the evacuation time, we need to choose a somewhat more complex plan (with a complexity of about 2200 rather than 2100). If we simplify plan any further, the evacuation time increases drastically rising from around 3000 to 7000. In addition, we see that the most reasonable plans are in the bottom-left of Pareto front in this graph.

Figure 4 shows the results when people could only use pedestrian paths. In this case, the lower bound on the evacuation time increased to 4500, but the plan complexity was similar to that in the previous case. Both Figs. 3 and 4 show that pedestrian simulations with multi-objective optimization can illustrate the clear trade-offs involved in selecting evacuation plans.

The characteristics of these trade-offs differ depending on the area features. In the case of Nishiyodogawa-ku, the structure formed relatively sharp 'L' shape, meaning that we could focus on the bottom-left region of the plot to find reasonable evacuation plans. However, if we conducted the same analysis for a different area, we could find a different structure. For example, Fig. 5 shows the analysis results for a different area. In this case, the shape of Pareto front has a more rounded shape, meaning that we would need to think more carefully about trade-off between simplicity and plan effectiveness in the evacuation. In some area, we might also need to introduce additional refuges to avoid such trade-offs. All this shows that such simulations can provide useful information for those making decisions about evacuation plans.

2.2   Evacuation Scalability Analysis

Another effective use-case of simulation for evacuation plan simulation is to classify the conditions resulting from particular disasters, as these can vary widely depending on the nature of the disaster, particularly for natural disasters. It is generally quite difficult to predict or estimate the conditions produced by a given disaster in detail disasters beforehand; therefore, we need to prepare response plans for a range of possibilities. However, it is not practical for first responders or ordinary people to prepare, learn, and execute a large number of different plans covering all possible conditions. To deal with this issue, we utilized evacuation simulations to classify a wide variety of possible conditions into a small number of categories where the same plan would be similarly effective.

For this study, we chose a part of Kamakura (Fig. 6) as the target area, as this is affected by large tsunamis immediately after large earthquake occur in the Nankai Trough. In this area, there are seven administrative zones and three

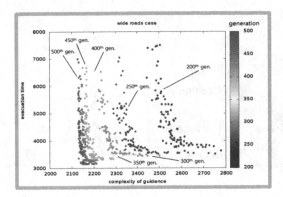

Fig. 3. Evacuation simulation results (with wide roads) (Color figure online)

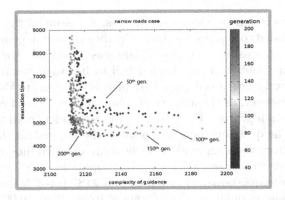

Fig. 4. Evacuation simulation results (narrow roads only)

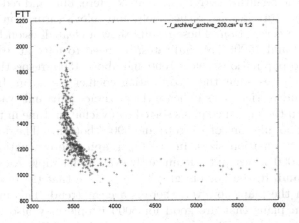

Fig. 5. Paleto solutions for another map

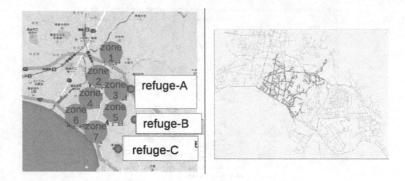

Fig. 6. Evacuation zones and refuges in Kamakura area.

official refuges. As in our previous experiments, we assumed that the people in each zone were guided to a particular refuge by the evacuation plan, meaning that the total number of possible evacuation plans was $3^7 = 2187$. For each scenario, we focused on the number of people that had to be evacuated from each area. If there are relatively few people, the best plan is for them to simply go to the nearest refuge. However, as the number of people increases, road congestion may hinder the evacuation process. In such cases, the responders need to guide people more carefully. The questions here are, what is the population threshold where we must switch from the simple plan to the more detailed one, and how many such detailed plans will be needed for a given population size?

To answer these questions, we simulated all 2187 possible evacuation plans for several different population sizes (ranging from 70 to 10,000), calculating the evacuation time correlation coefficients between each pair of populations. Figure 7 shows the resulting correlation matrix. Here, blue and red indicate positive and negative correlations, respectively, and color's saturation indicates the magnitude of the correlation. These results show a clear division between populations of 1000 and 1500. This indicates, we need to have at least two plans corresponding to populations below 1000 and above 1500, respectively.

Figure 8 illustrates what these correlation coefficients mean. In this graph, the horizontal and vertical axes indicate the guidance plan and evacuation time, respectively, with the guidance plans sorted by evacuation time in terms of their effectiveness for populations of 70 (top) and 5000 (bottom). The dot colors indicate the actual population sizes. In the top graph, the evacuation time for a population of 10000 varies quite significantly even with simple evacuation plans. On the other hand, in the bottom graph, we can see that the evacuation time still depends on the plan; however, there is a clear trend. This indicates that, while evacuation plans that are good for 5000 people may also work well for 10000, plans designed for 70 people may not work for 1000, with the boundary between the two categories falling between 1000 and 1500. If we study the correlation changes shown in Fig. 7 in more detail, we also find another weak boundary between 7000 and 9000. Although we should not determine the

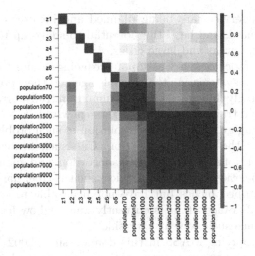

Fig. 7. Evacuation time correlations between populations of different sizes

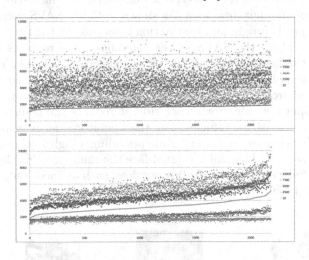

Fig. 8. Evacuation time variation for different plans, sorted by their results for populations of 70 (top) and 5000 (bottom).

number of population categories purely on the basis of such an analysis, this type of information will be useful for local governments and first responders helping them to prepare a variety of evacuation plans.

3 Transportation Simulations for On-Demand Traffic Systems

Traffic simulations can also be used to help evaluate novel transportation services. Due to the spread of mobile IT devices and the sharing economy, several new transportation services are being planned and introduced. These services are technology-oriented, and have the potential to shake up the transportation systems in both local areas and large cities.

Meanwhile, aging societies such as Japan are facing serious problems with their public transportation systems. As their people age and their populations drop, it is becoming increasingly difficult for them to maintain transportation service level for both residents and travelers. Therefore, these newly-developed transportation services are attracting great interest as a solution to such problems.

This leads us to the following question: Can such a novel transportation service replace traditional means of transportation and maintain the service levels in future as societies age? So far, services such as Uber has been successfully filling hitherto-untapped niches but have not been able to completely replace traditional modes of transport. It is currently unclear how feasible it would be to gradually introduce such systems city-side.

We have been applying MASS in this domain since 2002 [11,12], and have designed a demand-responsive transportation system called the Smart Access Vehicle Service (SAVS). SAVS is a type of taxi-sharing or dial-a-ride bus system, based on a simple fundamental idea. As shown in Fig. 9, SAVS users input their transportation needs (origin and destination locations) at the time when he/she wants to move. Then, the SAVS server combines these requests in real time and calculates the best way to assign the passengers to vehicles. To do this, it tries to assign a multiple users to the same vehicle if they are going in similar directions and share the vehicle. In this way SAVS has advantages for both user-side and operator-side. For a user-side, it reduces the transportation cost by enabling users to share vehicles. For the operator-side, it enables them to utilize their vehicles more effectively while providing a high level of door-to-door transportation service. That said, we still face the same question: Is SAVS more effective than traditional transportation services, such as fixed-route bus systems (FRBS) and taxi, and can it replace them?

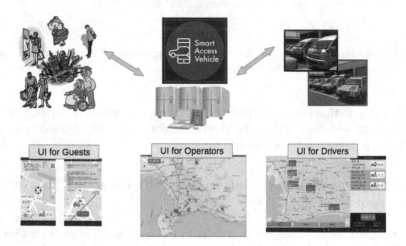

Fig. 9. SAVS system diagram.

When we began this study, we attempted to compare the effectiveness of SAVS with that of an FRBS, as FRBSs are the most popular services for every-day use. However, in aging societies, the decreasing number of users and the consequent reductions in frequency and routes of buses form a vicious cycle. To be a viable to alternative to such FBRS services, SAVS needs to demonstrate better performance in such circumstances.

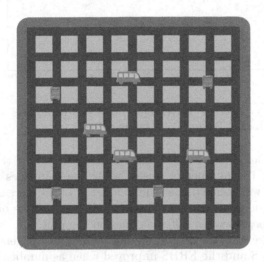

Fig. 10. Grid town used for SAVS simulations.

To compare these two services, we conducted simulation experiment based on a simple grid town, as shown in Fig. 10. Here, we assumed that the town's residents made random transport requests, whose origin and destination points were selected uniformly at random over the town. The town size was fixed, but the demand frequency was varied. To compare the performance of SAVS and the FBRS fairly, we tried to optimize the operation of both services. However, because these are hard optimization problems, we instead used semi-optimal solutions. For SAVS, we used the "successive best insertion" method, where each new request was assigned to the vehicle that could accept the new passenger with the least penalty to the already-assigned requests. For the FBRS, we applied GA to find the best possible set of routes for the town. Since this depends on the number of buses being used, we sought the best routes for several different numbers of buses.

In our simulations, we varied the number of buses and the demand frequency, calculating the average travel time for each passenger for both approaches under all test conditions. Here, we assumed that the FBRS would run on time, regardless of the number of passengers, meaning that the average travel time was not affected by the demand frequency. On the other hand, the SAVS travel time was quite sensitive to the demand frequency. Figure 11 shows the simulation results. Here, the horizontal and vertical axes indicate the number of buses and the average travel time, respectively. From a service usability viewpoint,

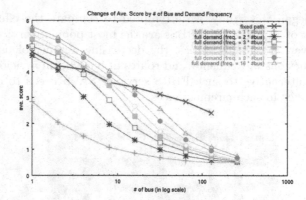

Fig. 11. Performance (Average Travel Time) of SAVS (thin lines) and FRBS (thick red line) versus Number of Buses (Color figure online)

lower travel times are better. The thick red line shows how the FRBS performance varied with the number of buses, while the thin lines show the SAVS results. For SAVS, we assumed that the number of buses increased according to the demand frequency, but considered several different ratios of the demand to the number of buses, shows as different lines on the plot.

From Fig. 11, we can see several significant points. In general, the performance of both SAVS and the FRBS improved when as number of buses operating increased. This makes sense, because operating more buses gives users more options (FRBS) and using more vehicle makes the service more flexible (SAVS). Another, more significant, feature is the travel time drops more rapidly with SAVS than with the FRBS. In all cases, the SAVS travel time quickly falling below that for the FRBS at a certain operation scale (number of buses). This means that, when there are sufficiently many users SAVS can perform better than the FRBS.

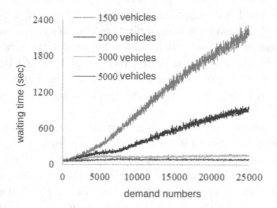

Fig. 12. Performance for Hakodate residents, for different numbers of vehicles

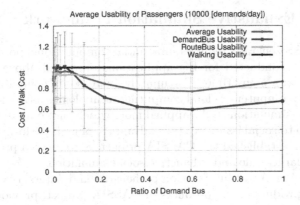

Fig. 13. Changes in travel time due to replacing a some bus services by SAVS in Hakodate City.

Based on these results, we developed a real SAVS system, as shown in Fig. 9, running several experimental and practical services [2, 7]. In these experiments, we also utilized simulation analysis to determine an appropriate operation scale (area covered and number of vehicles).

We also conducted several simulation analyses for possible future societies. For example, we imagined a scenario where all residents of Hakodate, a city with a population of about 300,000 and about 100,000 private cars, used SAVS instead of their own cars. Based on real person-trip data, we analyzed how the average waiting time per trip changed with the number of vehicle operated. Figure 12 shows the simulation results. These indicate that SAVS with 3,000 or 5,000 vehicles could operate with an average waiting time of less than 10 min. If we could realize the service on such a scale, we could drastically reduce the number of vehicles in the city, and completely eliminate traffic jams.

Next, we conducted a simulation analysis to evaluate effectiveness of gradually introducing SAVS to replace the current FRBS in Hakodate [4]. For this analysis, we removed some of the existing bus routes and introduced an equivalent SAVS to cover the demand for that area. Figure 13 shows the analysis results. This graph indicates that replacing about 60% of existing bus services would provide the best SAVS/FRBS mix, minimizing the travel time of bus users.

These results provide strong evidence that demand-responsive transportation such as SAVS could form a part of future transportation networks. Such analyses are only possible due to conducting large numbers of simulations under different conditions, which enables us to summarize the features of potential novel social services.

4 OACIS: Exhaustive Simulation Framework

Exhaustive MASS generally requires substantial computational power. For example, the analyses conducted for the applications described above required the simulation to be run many times. Fortunately, increases in computational power brought by supercomputer or cloud computing technologies have the potential to enable computer simulations to be applied more widely, not only to physical phenomena but also to social issues. To take advantage of high-performance computing resources, we established the CASSIA project [8,10], which provides several frameworks for large-scale and exhaustive social simulations.

The Organizing Assistant for Comprehensive and Interactive Simulations (OACIS) [6], a product of the products of CASSIA project, provides the ability to manage large numbers of simulation analysis jobs systematically and automatically. It is designed to handle exhaustive simulation analyses involving millions of runs. For such tasks, taking a naive manual approach to job management is both difficult and prone to human errors. In contrast, execution via OACIS is both stable and flexible, enabling researchers to conduct large-scale simulations in an efficient, reliable and reproducible way.

Figure 14 shows the OACIS system architecture. It was designed as a Web application built using the Ruby on Rails framework and provides both an interactive user interface and a batch-oriented command-line interface. When a user creates a job via the Web or a command-line interface, the application server creates a record of the job in the database. Another daemon process, "worker", manages a set of remote hosts (which we call "computational hosts"), running simulation jobs on these hosts by sending appropriate scripts to them over SSH. The worker also periodically checks the status of the submitted jobs and, when a job is complete, it downloads the results, stores them in the designated storage and database. The execution process is recorded in a traceable way to ensure

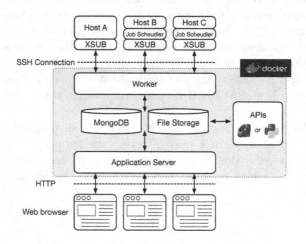

Fig. 14. Overview of the OACIS system.

reproducibility. A range of logs, including parameter values, execution dates, elapsed times, and simulator version numbers are automatically maintained, both in the database and on the file system. OACIS can handle wide range of different simulator types that can be run from the command-line.

OACIS also provides plug-in interface that gives us greater control mechanisms. For example, while default method of executing an OACIS project is to conduct fine-grained search of the whole parameter space, we can also introduce more intelligent methods of searching parameter space, such as GA, Bayesian optimization, and design-of-experiment as plug-in modules. Currently OACIS accepts modules written in the Ruby or Python programming languages. The evacuation planning application (Sect. 2.1) is a typical example of plug-in usage.

We believe that exhaustive MASS management tool such as OACIS will be one of the keys to making MASS practical for real applications. OACIS is available as open-source software under an MIT license (http://github.com/crest-cassia/oacis).

5   Concluding Remarks

Exhaustive simulation and analysis are a fundamental utilizing MASS for practical applications. As the three example applications in this article illustrate, exhaustive MASS can illustrate the features of social phenomena from several different points of view. As part of the CASSIA project, we have also worked on other MASS applications, such as stock market [5,14,17] and general traffic simulations [13].

Historically, one drawback of exhaustive MASS has been that it requires enormous computational power. Fortunately, recent progress in computer device and HPC technology has enabled such a brute-force approach to become practical. We have previously investigated the relationship between HPC progress and MASS applications, drawing up MASS and HPC roadmaps [9]. According to these roadmaps, it will soon be possible to apply exhaustive MASS approach at an even larger scale, such as simulating traffic across metropolis.

At some point in the future, we may develop more feasible and accurate models for simulating human and social behaviors, but, this is likely to take several decades. Until then, we believe exhaustive MASS will become the dominant approach to computational social science.

Acknowledgement. The authors acknowledges partial support from MEXT as part of the "Exploratory Challenges on Post-K computer (Studies of multi-level spatiotemporal simulation of socioeconomic phenomena)". This research used the computational resources of the K computer provided by the RIKEN Center for Computational Science through the HPCI System Research project (Project ID: hp170266 and hp170345).

References

1. Deb, K., Agrawal, S., Pratap, A., Meyarivan, T.: A fast elitist non-dominated sorting genetic algorithm for multi-objective optimization: NSGA-II. In: Schoenauer, M., et al. (eds.) PPSN 2000. LNCS, vol. 1917, pp. 849–858. Springer, Heidelberg (2000). https://doi.org/10.1007/3-540-45356-3_83
2. Nakashima, H., et al.: One cycle of smart access vehicle service development. In: Maeno, T., Sawatani, Y., Hara, T. (eds.) Serviceology for Designing the Future, pp. 287–295. Springer, Tokyo (2014). https://doi.org/10.1007/978-4-431-55861-3_17
3. Kobayashi, K., Narisawa, R., Yasui, Y., Fujisawa, K.: Experimental analyses of the evacuation planning model using lexicographically quickest flow (in japanese). Trans. Oper. Res. Soc. Jpn. **59**, 86–105 (2016). https://doi.org/10.15807/torsj.59.86
4. Miyachi, M., Noda, I.: Evaluation method for gradual introduction of demand-responsible public transportation system by simulation. In: Proceedings of WSSIT. ICS1, March 2015
5. Mizuta, T., Kosugi, S., Kusumoto, T., Matsumoto, W., Izumi, K.: Effects of dark-pools on financial markets' efficiency and price discovery function: aninvestigation by multi-agent simulations. Evol. Inst. Econ. Rev. **12**(2), 375–394 (2015). https://doi.org/10.1007/s40844-015-0020-3
6. Murase, Y., Uchitane, T., Ito, N.: A tool for parameter-space explorations. Phys. Procedia **57**, 73–76 (2014)
7. Nakashima, H., et al.: Design of the smart access vehicle system with large scale MA simulation. In: Proceedings of the 1st International Workshop on Multiagent-based Societal Systems (MASS 2013), May 2013
8. Noda, I.: Project CASSIA: framework for administration of social simulations on massively parallel computers. In: Proceedings ofd ATIP workshop 2014 in SC14, November 2014
9. Noda, I., Ito, N., Izumi, K., Mizuta, H., Kamada, T., Hattori, H.: Roadmap and research issues of multiagent social simulation using high-performance computing. J. Comput. Soc. Sci. **1**(1), 155–166 (2018)
10. Noda, I., et al.: Roadmap for multiagent social simulation on HPC. In: Kurihara, S., Hattori, H. (eds.) Proceedings of DOCMAS-WEIN 2015, December 2015
11. Noda, I., Masayuki, O., Kumada, Y., Nakashima, H.: Usability of dial-a-ride systems. In: Proceedings of AAMAS-2005, p. 726, July 2005
12. Ohta, M., Shinoda, K., Noda, I., Kurumatani, K., Nakashima, H.: Usability of demand-bus in town area. Technical report 2002-ITS-11-33, vol. 2002, no. 115, ISSN 0919–6072, Reports of ITS meeting in IPSJ, November 2002
13. Osogami, T., et al.: IBM mega traffic simulator. IBM Res. Dev. J. (2013). RT0896
14. Torii, T., Izumi, K., Yamada, K.: Shock transfer by arbitrage trading: analysis using multi-asset artificial market. Evol. Inst. Econ. Rev. **12**(2), 395–412 (2016)
15. Yamashita, T., Okada, T., Noda, I.: Implementation of simulation environment for exhaustive analysis of huge-scale pedestrian flow. SICE JCMSI **6**(2), 137–146 (2013)
16. Yamashita, T., Soeda, S., Onishi, M., Noda, I.: Development and application of high-speed evacuation simulator with one-dimensional pedestrian model. J. Inf. Process. Soc. Jpn. **53**(7), 1732–1744 (2012)
17. Yonenoh, H., Izumi, K.: Destabilization effect of var-based risk management on a multiple-asset market: An artificial market approach. In: 23rd International Symposium on Artificial Life and Robotics (AROB 2018) (2018)

Inverse Reinforcement Learning for Agents Behavior in a Crowd Simulator

Nahum Alvarez(✉) and Itsuki Noda

The National Institute of Advanced Industrial Science and Technology (AIST),
Tokyo, Japan
{nahum.alvarez,i.noda}@aist.go.jp

Abstract. Crowd behavior has been subject of study due to its applications in fields like disaster evacuation, smart town planning and business strategic placing. However, obtaining patterns from the crowd to make a working model is difficult, as it requires an enormous quantity of data from observation and analysis and is impractical in many scenarios due to logistic and legal issues. Machine learning techniques are a good tool to overcome these difficulties, using a relatively small training data set to identify patterns, allowing crowd agents to react to similar situations accordingly. We implemented a behavioral agent model that uses such techniques into a large-scale crowd simulator, and apply inverse reinforcement learning to adjust agents' behaviors by examples. The goal of the system is to provide to the agents a realistic behavior model and a method to orient themselves without knowing the scenario's layout, based in learnt patterns around environment features.

Keywords: Pedestrian simulation · Inverse reinforcement learning · Multi-agent systems

1 Introduction

Crowd movement is a topic whose study has a large number of applications in diverse domains. Naturally, to experimenting or testing scenarios with real people presents a number of logistic problems and is generally not practical, or even infeasible in certain instances. Therefore, a widely accepted solution is to use a simulator to replicate the desired scenario. Then, the simulation can be used for extracting crowd behavior patterns and predicting its movement. This could help in improving our understanding of real life tasks like city planning, disaster prevention, or business strategy. Agent based models are commonly used to perform the simulations, due to its flexibility and scalability, and allow to produce complex crowd interactions using simple action patterns. However, human behavior is a factor difficult to model: people's actions are goal-driven but those goals are not usually visible and do not follow optimized plans often. Also, scalability and performance requirements arise when we need to work in scenarios involving large numbers of humans, so even basic behaviors pose a

© Springer Nature Switzerland AG 2019
D. Lin et al. (Eds.): MMAS 2018, LNAI 11422, pp. 81–95, 2019.
https://doi.org/10.1007/978-3-030-20937-7_6

challenge to researchers. A possible way to solve this problem is to use machine learning techniques on available similar data in order to give the agents a way to react to new situations.

In this paper, we present a model that includes the use of inverse reinforcement learning (IRL from here on) for the agents' decision making process, training them with knowledge learnt from previous data. The context of our research lies in the domain of pedestrian simulation on cities, with the objective of extracting knowledge of the pedestrian flow around concrete points of the map that contain certain features, like shops or restaurants, and predicting which places are more appropriate for certain business. We aim to deploy a large number of agents with different profiles depending of their goal (shopping, work, entertainment) and observe how their behavior is influenced by the features in the environment. With this information we would be able to decide which spot is best for certain type of feature and how would change pedestrian affluence if we add new features or modify the existent ones. This is done by analyzing the crowd movement flow according of map features and agent characteristics. Previously IRL techniques has been used to calculate trajectories and plan movements, but as far as we know its use in agents based simulators or feature map optimization has been sparse.

We developed a crowd simulator designed to generate pedestrian movement in city scenarios using real world city maps that originally used simple scripted agents to calculate trajectories, and we expanded it by adding a behavior module that works with IRL and is used by the agents to decide which path take. The decision process is influenced by the preexistent features in the map generating similar behavior for places with similar features. This module also allows the agents to traverse maps whose layout is not known. Also, once they have learned behavior patterns related to the map features, they can be put on a different map and behave the same way they did in the original scenario.

The rest of the present document is organized as follows: Sect. 2 contains a review of previous work on reinforcement learning used for agent behavior and pedestrian simulators and the techniques they use. Section 3 describes in detail our crowd simulator and its architecture, and Sect. 4 presents our agent model and the IRL method that generate their behavior. Section 5 contains the tests we performed to validate the system and the results we obtained from them. Finally Sect. 6 contains the conclusions of our research.

2   Related Work

Crowd simulation have been recently the object of rising interest because it can deal with a number of important problems in our society. For example, traffic simulation can be used to improve transportation systems and networks, and also in obtaining solutions to lowering car pollution [6]. Pedestrian simulation is useful to design evacuation strategies and identifying potential problems in concrete scenarios like natural disasters or terrorist incidents, like [22] or [12]. In these works we can see that not only an accurate model is needed, but a high degree of scalability is mandatory, as simulating hundred of thousands people requires many resources in terms of computational power. Different models has been used to achieve efficient and accurate simulations: for example, [3] shows the simulation of the crowd flow in a train station during an event using the Cellular Automata model, or our own system that uses the Social Force model described in [7]. However, every model has certain limitations, like the Social Force model having issues representing realistic collision behavior at high densities due to the specification of the repulsive interaction forces, or the Cellular Automata model having issues at modeling agents at high or non homogeneous velocities [17]. Solutions of these shortcomings have been proposed by extending the models, often making them domain-specific to some degree. For example, the Social Force model was upgraded in [9] to describe detailed velocity control of pedestrians, and other works like [23] and [11] add a collision-prediction/-avoidance force model.

There is another topic where pedestrian simulators can be applied, which is the one we are interested in: city and business location planning. We want to analyze people movements and behavior in their daily city life, obtaining insight of what places attract more people and how different types of locations affect their actions. Then, once we have a model of the patterns that people follow, we could simulate them in other environments to assess the effectiveness of certain spots, or predict how a future potential business or facility could perform at different locations. We are interested in such kind of application and it is the objective of the present work.

Aiming to that goal, we developed CrowdWalk, a crowd simulator that uses a multi-agent model to represent pedestrians. Using agents is a popular approach due to be able of generate complex behavior with simple agent design and also escalates well, being appropriate for large scenarios. There are a wide range of works in pedestrian simulation with agents, using different techniques. Systems based in video analysis work well, like the one in [24], but in order to remain practical it narrows their domain, using tile location and pre-generated trajectories. Another common strategy is to model the agents with a dual behavior system controlling two types of movement (or behavior): micro and macro movement. The first deals with collision avoiding in the near space and adjusting the agent's velocity in the crowd's flow, and the second is the one in charge of driving the agent towards its goal, creating and updating its route and taking care of the decision making process [21]. Our simulator handles micro movements in an autonomous way, with its own subsystem where agents adapt to the crowd flow, and also allows to control macro movements using behavior scripts. To achieve our goal, we are focused in macro movements as it is the module that creates the agent's behavior.

However, a basic action for an agent macro movement like calculating the most optimal route to a goal in a crowded scenario is a complex task: an a priori calculated optimal route can become much slower if an enough large number of agents take it, and this is the simplest problem that could arise; nevertheless, this is not what we intend as we only aim to replicate pedestrian behavior. Learning such behavior patterns is an interesting question: humans usually do not take the most optimal route, and even congestion can be seen as a positive factor ("if there are many people, is because is good") as noted by [4]. In such kind of domains, we can take advantage of machine learning techniques. Concretely, apprenticeship learning methods have been widely used in intelligent agents' systems to train them to perform tasks in changing environments like [18] or [20]. As we noted, simulating people's behavior and not only trajectory planning is a difficult task, as their movements are governed by hidden rules and oriented to goals that may be hidden as well. We can observe strategies to emulate different behaviors for agents in [6] but it is a static model with pre-designed driving styles, having the problem of not being able to simulate unplanned behaviors. There are previous works where agents are given a behavior cognitive model for pedestrians like in [14,15] or [4], but they are specific to its domain, escalating badly, or they take as a given the reward or utility functions that drive the agents behavior, which often is unknown in complex scenarios. Using IRL is appropriate to overcome this issue, because IRL methods work on domains where the reward function is hidden. Hence, it is ideal to model animals and humans behavior [16]. Interestingly, the works that use IRL to manage agent's behavior are sparse, but are recently some works are starting to use it [19]. IRL not only allows to train agents into achieving concrete goals, but also can learn different behavior patterns, as it is shown in [1] where driving styles are learned by an agent. There are a number of algorithms to solve IRL problems, like the ones in [8] or [10]. We decided to use the maximum entropy approach [25] because it works well when we do not have much information about the solution space, as we are dealing with city scenarios with a layout a priori unknown by the agents. There are methods that perform better, like [5] which it works on a subset of MDP, but it does not match well with our domain, or [13] which could be interesting to apply in future instances of our research.

3   Pedestrian Simulator

CrowdWalk is a pedestrian simulator we developed to perform crowd behavior prediction in disaster scenarios in order to identify potential bottleneck issues when coordinating evacuation routes. Aside of this type of scenarios, CrowdWalk was actually designed for generic uses, so it is possible to create pedestrian simulation with other purposes. In CrowdWalk, each agent (pedestrian) walks on a map toward its own goal. It can simulate movements of more than 1 million agents in a large area like complex building or town blocks in a city. Maps and agents' behaviors are configurable so that we can conduct simulations with various situations of maps and policies of agents. The architecture of CrowdWalk is depicted in Fig. 1, and shows its principal work modules. We omitted from the diagram the modules related to the IRL process as in this section we want to describe in depth the application where we built learning agents on. We will focus in the IRL process flow and the new agents with detail in the next section. First, CrowdWalk has two main working modules: an Agent handler and the Simulation

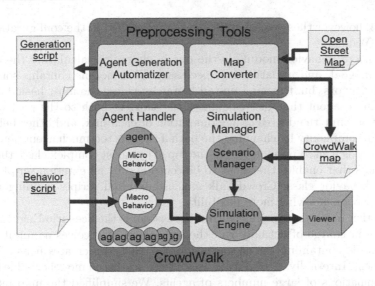

Fig. 1. The architecture diagram of CrowdWalk. It has two main modules: one managing the agents and other in charge of the environment simulation. Each one of these modules is configured by different files containing the specifications of the simulations. Some of those files can be automatized using the system preprocessing tools to some extent for easier construction.

manager. The Agent handler contains an agent factory, that generates one agent per pedestrian. Each agent contains its own decision model that its composed by the micro and macro behavior modules. The micro behavior module in each agent takes care of micro movements automatically, calculating when an agent has to stop, walk slower or even try take other route due to be unable to continue its original path. However, the final decision of selecting other path is left to the macro behavior module, and actually, the macro behavior module is able to override any orders from the micro movements module if deems so. The speed of an agent is given in relation with the density of the link he is currently in, being slower as the link is more crowded, until a maximum capacity limit where it is not possible to continue advancing. Concretely, it is determined according to the social force model as following:

$$\frac{dv_i}{dt} = A_0 \left(v_i^* - v_i\right) - A_1 \sum_{j \in H_i} \exp\left(A_2 \left(s - \|p_i - p_j\|\right)\right)$$

where v_i, v_i^* and p_i is the current and max speed, and the current location of agent i, respectively. §H_i is the set of agents located in front of the agent i. And s is the radius of a personal space. A_0, A_1 and A_2 are constant parameters whose purpose is to adjust the formula. Through experimental observations in real scenarios we set these parameters, the personal space radius and the max speed to a default of $A_0 = 0.962$, $A_1 = 0.869$, $A_2 = 4.682$, $v_i^* = 1.023$ and

$s = 1.044$, however these parameters can be customized in the configuration files of CrowdWalk.

The macro behavior module is the one in charge of calculating the agent's route to its goal, and updating it if necessary. This module contains some predefined behaviors, built using a nested hierarchy where the most basic behavior consists in an agent that just calculates the shortest path to the goal without taking in account the degree of agglomeration of each link, and other behaviors increase in complexity by changing the path if there is too much agent density, or avoiding roads it used previously. On the top of the most complex class, there is a special class that enables the agent to be controlled by an external script. Using this last behavior class, CrowdWalk can use external scripts defining agent's macro behavior, allowing more flexibility.

The other important module within the system is the Scenario Engine, which is the one in charge of actually run the simulation. It receives as input a configuration file containing the scenario information and recreates it as a virtual environment. Internally, CrowdWalk uses a Network-based model capable of high speed simulations of large numbers of agents. We simplified the map into a 1-dimensional network consists of nodes and links instead of 2D free space. Our main focus is to investigate phenomena and behaviors of a large scale crowd in a large area, so we need to execute exhaustive simulations with a large number of configurations. Therefore, we chose a light computational 1D model rather than a 2D model one. However, it is capable of simulate 3-dimensional structures as well, being capable of representing the internal layout of a building.

CrowdWalk uses five configuration files to setup simulation environments. The five files are described as follows:

Properties file: specifies top-level configurations of the simulation. Other configuration files listed below are specified in this file.

Map file: specifies a map for the simulation.

Generation file: specifies the rules to generate agents. Each generation rule specify agent classes, other parameters like the max speed and personal space radius, populations, goals, and generation time independently.

Scenario file: specifies a sequence of events occur during the simulation.

Fallback file: specifies the default values for the simulation parameters, like the ones in the social force model.

The model of the map consists in a custom xml that describes the map in the form of a road network represented by nodes (intersections) and links (road path) composing a graph. A link has a length (how long agents need to walk from a end to another) and width (how many agents can walk in parallel), and can be two-way or one-way. Nodes and links can have *tags* as labels to indicate goals and other features information, like what kind of facilities are on that location. The xml model can be created automatically using a tool included in CrowdWalk that converts maps obtained from the open source software Open Street Map[1] into our custom format. This allows us to use any possible city map in the world with no additional effort.

---

[1] https://www.openstreetmap.org.

The agent generation script is a file containing the rules of agent generation, i.e. what number of agents are created, which type of agents will be and if they are not any default type, which agent behavior file the system will use, which point they come from, and which point they are going to. CrowdWalk also has a tool to automatically generate this file by providing some simple rules and the map model. Finally, the agent behavior is contained in a script and describes the macro behavior of the agent. This script optional, as there are a number of predefined agents, like agents that move randomly, or agents that move directly towards their goal. For our current research we created an IRL agent we will describe in depth in the next section.

The Agent handler is called by the Simulation manager in order to generate the agents in the virtual environment following the rules given in the agent generation script. When running, the simulation engine represents the scenario as a graphic simulation where the agents will behave according to each one's own behavior modules, allowing pausing the simulation at any moment and inspecting every element part of it (like the current internal state of any agent, and any node or link).

Once CrowdWalk is running it shows a simulation of the agents traversing the city map until all the agents reach their goal point; When the agents are walking freely they are colored green, but when they have to stop or walk slower they become red, showing bottlenecks in the map. The simulator screen allows to pause the simulation and examine every agent, map node or link information. The simulation is run at accelerated time, but it shows the real world time it is taking given the velocity of the agents. When finished, it records each agent path in a log with timestamps for posterior replication or analysis purposes.

4 Agent Model

IRL techniques work on domains that can be modeled by a Markov decision process (MDP, from here on after) and are used to learn its hidden reward function. MDP are defined by a tuple M = {S, $\mathcal{A}$, $\mathcal{T}$, γ, r}, where S is the state space of the model, $\mathcal{A}$ is the set of actions that can be performed, $\mathcal{T}$ is the transition function, which returns the probability of transition from one state to other given a concrete action, and usually is given in the form of a matrix, r is the reward function that generates a reward value from reaching a state, and γ is a discount factor, that applies when calculating accumulated reward through consecutive actions. When working with models with an unknown reward function, IRL methods provide us a way to obtain it. In order to get r, it is also provided a set of expert trajectories T, consisting of "paths" composed of pairs of states and actions.

We developed an automatic module that converts the city map used in CrowdWalk into a MDP, ready to be used by our IRL method. This tool translates map nodes into states, and creates a possible action for each link that it has. Also, in order to optimize the model, all the nodes that only have two links are trimmed, as there are no other possible decisions once a pedestrian enter in one other than continue walking or going back. Once we have the MDP model for the map, we run the CrowdWalk IRL module, that consists on an instance of the IRL algorithm, using a modified version of the maximum entropy method found in [2]. We adapted this module in order to use a variable number of possible actions on each state, as each map node has a different number of possible links to take. The input of this module is the MDP representing the current map, and a file containing the training trajectories we want to train. It is possible to run this process using trajectories for each available behavior we want to train, but also we can run it only once training all the behaviors at the same time. For example, we can train shopping behavior using routes that go to the shops on the map, preferring shops hubs like malls or shops surrounded by other entertainment facilities, or business behavior by training the routes that working people would do, preferring wide avenues over small and crowded streets; we can do this once per each behavior or put together all of the trajectories and train them as a whole. The resulting product of the module is a file containing the optimal policy function derived from the reward function generated by the IRL algorithm. This policy function takes the form of a lookup table stored in a file, which will be used by the system's agents. All of these actions are performed before the simulation is executed as a pre-processing task. Thus, even if this pipeline can take a long time depending of the complexity of the map (about one hour for a map for one Tokyo district, with around 2000 nodes), it does not represent a big impact in the simulation speed as the policy selection once we have this file is enough to use it in real time. The process flow once included in the architecture we explained in the previous section is depicted in Fig. 2.

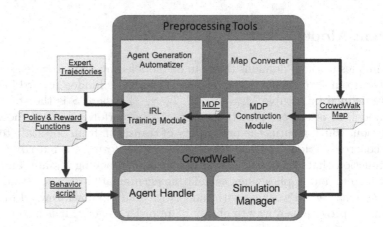

Fig. 2. The IRL process integrated in the system. We added two extra modules to the system in order to create a MDP based in the simulated scenario and train the agents with expert trajectories. This pipeline integrates naturally with the architecture of the system.

As we described in the previous section, when a simulation runs in Crowd-Walk, the agents have a macro behavior module which is in charge of the decision making process by selecting a type of behavior for the agents. We developed a type of agent, called IRL agent, that works with an input behavior script and the IRL's resulting policy and decides which link to take on the probabilities contained in it. The behavior script contains a list of goals, which describes the features the agent wants to visit. They can be generic (like "visiting three restaurants") or a concrete one (like "visiting the restaurant located in the node labeled as nd00327"). Each goal in the list also contains the conditions for its satisfaction, which can be reaching the goal, staying in the goal a defined time, reaching a number of goals of that type (in case of the generic goal), or a combination of them. Also, the script contains an evacuation point, where the agent will go after completing its goals. The agent has access to the optimal policy learned from the IRL process (stored as a lookup table), and also the set of rules contained in its behavior script, whose decision making process is shown in Fig. 3. The agent starts in an state called "wandering". In this state, on each map node, the agent obtains from the policy table a list containing the probabilities of taking each one of the available links on that node. Then the agent chooses which path it will take based on that probability list. Whenever the agent visits a goal node it checks and updates its satisfaction conditions. If that goal is satisfied, the agent enter briefly into another state, called "pathfinder", which makes it go to its next goal using the most optimal path. However, it leaves this state as soon as it has left the featured area containing the previous goal, and returns to "wandering". The agents decide they left the area of a goal by have a distance threshold from the goal they are leaving.

The rationale behind the pathfinder state is to avoid returning to the previously visited nodes (on a side note, goals already visited do not count when returning to them), as the nearly policies would drive back the agent to them. Currently this is controlled by the distance threshold, but in future installments of the system we will use multiple policy functions with a smart selection method between them. Once all the goals have been completed, the agent enters again in "pathfinder" mode and goes straightly to its evacuation point, leaving the map.

5   Preliminary Validation

We performed a preliminary set of tests to validate two aspects of our method: first, if the intended behavior is observed in the agents, and how the policy and reward values are distributed on a featured map, and second, that the agents are capable to reach their goal points. Additionally, we aimed to identify unpredicted issues and deviations from our expectations.

First, we selected a map from a portion of Tokyo containing commercial areas, touristic spots, a train station, and residential zones. In the map there were a total of 36 features, which we classified in three groups: shops, restaurants or entertainment. We generated by hand 3000 routes representing pedestrians making errands (we observed in previous tests that training that number of

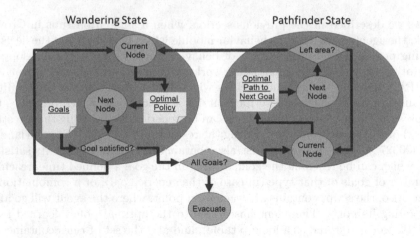

Fig. 3. The algorithm followed by the IRL agents: once they reach a map node, they use the optimal policy function to choose the next node they will go to. If they satisfy a goal, they leave the area and start wandering again. Also they check their list of goals and leave the map when all of them were visited.

sample routes results in a better performance than using bigger data sets). The routes start on 20 random points in the map, covering a 60% of it (a bit more, they cover 165 nodes from 273) and evacuate on a designated area. We are aware that for a complete validation we will need to use trajectory data from real humans. However, we are expecting to obtain a data set containing pedestrian behavior from other domains, like a department store or a fireworks festival, so we will adapt our simulator to represent these new environments and perform more definitive tests.

We prepared two different maps for training the routes: one was designed to train only shopping patterns; i.e. we deleted from the map any feature not classified as shop. The second map was prepared using the original, containing all three groups of features. We trained the routes in these two maps, and generated two different optimal policy files. Figure 4 depicts how the rewards influence in the map. Links in red have a probability greater than 80% to be selected as the next path, in yellow when is between 40% and 80%, and in green when it is lower than 40% but greater than 20%. As we can see in the figure, training with three groups of features generates new colored links but also increases the probability of taking the links in areas where different features are contained. We want to note that colored links appear over the whole map, and not only in the areas where routes were trained.

Then, we performed three different sets of simulations using 3000, 6000 and 10000 IRL agents with the two different policy files. The agents start from 20 different random points and have a goal of visit 4 featured spots. Also, in order to compare the agents behavior, we performed a parallel simulation using other type of agent called "pathfinder agent", capable of calculate optimal routes and going directly to its goals (so it is always in the pathfinder state), as we wanted to compare our theoretically more realistic behavior with an agent capable of reaching scripted route points. We designed routes for these agents placing waypoints on certain featured areas (but not in feature spots); the agents are programmed to walk to those points in order and then evacuate at the final point.

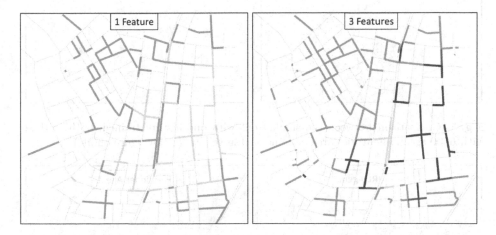

Fig. 4. The rewarded links in the map when training with one and three different types of features. The links are colored depending of their reward value, with no coloring in case of no reward, green if there is a low reward, yellow if it is moderate and red for high rewards. (Color figure online)

All the simulations showed similar results in terms of population in featured areas and number of features visited. In Fig. 5 we can observe the distribution of the pedestrians in the simulation of 6000 agents with only one feature group trained. The pathfinder agents crowd around the waypoints, but since they are programmed to only follow the best path, they avoid other similar featured areas that are not part of it. They also concentrate in other areas that do not contain such features, but are just the optimal path to the goal (for example, the big avenue that runs vertically across the map, which is a navigational hub). On the other hand, IRL agents tend to disperse themselves when they are not in featured areas. Figure 6 shows a caption of the simulation with the three types of featured areas marked with different colors. IRL agents populate almost all of the featured areas, but as the agents have a much more varied featured-driven behavior, the crowd in some of them is not as clear-cut as the in the first experiment.

We also extracted population density data from our tests with the full features in the map. The IRL agents visited all the 36 featured nodes in the map, with an average of 7.11 featured spots, whilst the pathfinder agents visited an average of 2.23, leaving 9 nodes that were untouched by them. Naturally, the pathfinder agents only went to the featured nodes that were by chance in their path to the goal, but, interestingly this means that not all business are in the most optimal paths and agents that does not take in account behavioral patterns, will ignore places that may be important. Finally, we observed space to

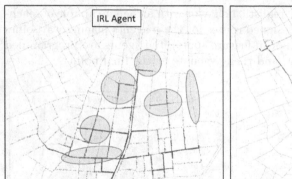
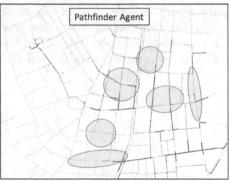

Fig. 5. Comparison between the simulations with one feature trained, both of them with 6000 agents. Featured areas are marked in yellow. (Color figure online)

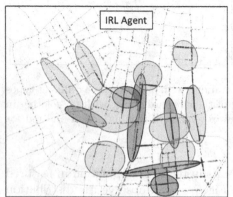
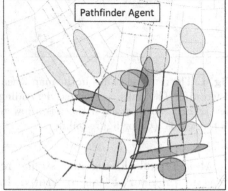

Fig. 6. Comparison between the behavior of the agents used in a simulation with the three groups of features trained, both of them with 6000 agents. The colors used mark different areas: yellow for shops, blue for restaurants, and green for entertainment. (Color figure online)

improvement, identifying a number of issues in the IRL agents. First, we noticed deadlocks emerging when there are a high number of agents, and we plan to solve that problem in the next version of the system; however, the deadlocks appear much more often using pathfinder agents. We will add reactive behavior to the agents in order make them able to detect when they cannot continue their path and even warn other agents of it.

Also, we think we could improve the agents behavior when shifting between behavior patterns, because currently switching behaviors is predefined and we think that is more a way to circumvent the fact that the agents still do not switch policy functions (and even it may not be suitable to real situations). We plan to perform an additional layer of learning to obtain a cognitive model for changing behaviors from the data used for training, and then we can manage different policies for different behaviors. Once we finish this behavior management method, we will test if its better to have one unique policy and reward functions for multiple trained behaviors, or to maintain one per behavior, shifting the policy depending of the goal.

6 Conclusions

In this paper we presented an agent-based pedestrian simulator that uses inverse reinforcement learning in order to imitate behavior patterns learned from expert's trajectories. Current pedestrian or crowd simulators rarely use this approach in order to simulate the crowd behavior, preferring to use this method for optimal trajectory generation instead. However, such kind of system would have a wide array of applications in fields: for example it can be used for smart city planning by extracting the movement patterns of pedestrians and applying those patterns to create optimal paths to key areas; it can be used for disaster prevention by identifying which areas are more likely to create bottlenecks in evacuations, and avoid undesirable paths that would be nonetheless taken by fleeing pedestrians; it also can be applied to take business strategy decisions in where to place certain types of business by predicting how they can perform in attracting customers depending of their surrounding features.

We developed a module that provides behavioral learning to the agents in our crowd simulator. This module works using an inverse reinforcement learning technique by converting the domain of pedestrians walking across a city into a Markov decision process. We performed two sets of experiments obtaining promising results when replicating the intended behavior. Our IRL agents visit spots in the map that are ignored by agents that only calculate the most optimal route to the goal, generating better behavior. Also, by observing the reward values of the links on the map we can detect which places are more optimal for certain business. We observed interesting aspects in our tests. First, when the number of agents increase, pedestrian congestion was much more common with pathfinder agents than using the IRL agents, hindering their performance or even generating deadlocks at certain junctions. This is mostly due to the wandering nature of the IRL agents around zones that match their behavior pattern but are not part of optimal paths. We also observed that IRL agents have a consistent behavior independently of the number of simulated agents.

In the next steps of our research, we plan to improve the agents with further machine learning techniques, in order to teach them when to switch between different behavior patterns. We also plan to validate the behavior of our agents by comparing them with live data from real pedestrians. In order to do this and due to difficulties to track effectively massive numbers of people, we will apply our system to concrete environments more manageable, like crowd movement in controlled events or customer behavior inside of supermarkets. We think IRL techniques opened an interesting path that was not enough explored although they are well known from long ago, maybe because a lack of simulation technology. Thus, we aim to provide better understanding of crowd simulation using IRL and usable tools for its potential applications.

References

1. Abbeel, P., Ng, A.Y.: Apprenticeship learning via inverse reinforcement learning. In: Proceedings of the Twenty-First International Conference on Machine Learning, p. 1. ACM (2004)
2. Alger, M.: Deep inverse reinforcement learning (2015)
3. Crociani, L., Lämmel, G., Vizzari, G.: Multi-scale simulation for crowd management: a case study in an urban scenario. In: Osman, N., Sierra, C. (eds.) AAMAS 2016. LNCS (LNAI), vol. 10002, pp. 147–162. Springer, Cham (2016). https://doi.org/10.1007/978-3-319-46882-2_9
4. Crociani, L., Vizzari, G., Yanagisawa, D., Nishinari, K., Bandini, S.: Route choice in pedestrian simulation: design and evaluation of a model based on empirical observations. Intell. Artif. **10**(2), 163–182 (2016)
5. Dvijotham, K., Todorov, E.: Inverse optimal control with linearly-solvable MDPs. In: Proceedings of the 27th International Conference on Machine Learning (ICML 2010), pp. 335–342 (2010)
6. Faccin, J., Nunes, I., Bazzan, A.: Understanding the behaviour of learning-based BDI agents in the Braess' paradox. In: Berndt, J.O., Petta, P., Unland, R. (eds.) MATES 2017. LNCS (LNAI), vol. 10413, pp. 187–204. Springer, Cham (2017). https://doi.org/10.1007/978-3-319-64798-2_12
7. Helbing, D., Molnar, P.: Social force model for pedestrian dynamics. Phys. Rev. E **51**(5), 4282–4286 (1995)
8. Herman, M., Gindele, T., Wagner, J., Schmitt, F., Quignon, C., Burgard, W.: Learning high-level navigation strategies via inverse reinforcement learning: a comparative analysis. In: Kang, B.H., Bai, Q. (eds.) AI 2016. LNCS (LNAI), vol. 9992, pp. 525–534. Springer, Cham (2016). https://doi.org/10.1007/978-3-319-50127-7_45
9. Johansson, A., Helbing, D., Shukla, P.K.: Specification of the social force pedestrian model by evolutionary adjustment to video tracking data. Adv. Complex Syst. **10**(2), 271–288 (2007). https://doi.org/10.1142/S0219525907001355
10. Kohjima, M., Matsubayashi, T., Sawada, H.: What-if prediction via inverse reinforcement learning. In: Proceedings of the Thirtieth International Florida Artificial Intelligence Research Society Conference, FLAIRS 2017, Marco Island, Florida, USA, 22–24 May 2017, pp. 74–79 (2017). https://aaai.org/ocs/index.php/FLAIRS/FLAIRS17/paper/view/15503
11. Lämmel, G., Plaue, M.: Getting out of the way: collision-avoiding pedestrian models compared to the RealWorld. In: Weidmann, U., Kirsch, U., Schreckenberg, M. (eds.) Pedestrian and Evacuation Dynamics 2012, pp. 1275–1289. Springer, Cham (2014). https://doi.org/10.1007/978-3-319-02447-9_105
12. Lämmel, G., Grether, D., Nagel, K.: The representation and implementation of time-dependent inundation in large-scale microscopic evacuation simulations. Transp. Res. Part C Emerg. Technol. **18**(1), 84–98 (2010)
13. Levine, S., Popovic, Z., Koltun, V.: Nonlinear inverse reinforcement learning with Gaussian processes. In: Advances in Neural Information Processing Systems, pp. 19–27 (2011)
14. Luo, L., et al.: Agent-based human behavior modeling for crowd simulation. Comput. Animat. Virtual Worlds **19**(3–4), 271–281 (2008)
15. Martinez-Gil, F., Lozano, M., Fernández, F.: Emergent behaviors and scalability for multi-agent reinforcement learning-based pedestrian models. Simul. Model. Pract. Theory **74**, 117–133 (2017)

16. Ng, A.Y., Russell, S.J., et al.: Algorithms for inverse reinforcement learning. In: ICML, pp. 663–670 (2000)
17. Schadschneider, A., Klingsch, W., Klüpfel, H., Kretz, T., Rogsch, C., Seyfried, A.: Evacuation dynamics: empirical results, modeling and applications. In: Meyers, R. (ed.) Extreme Environmental Events, pp. 517–550. Springer, New York (2011). https://doi.org/10.1007/978-1-4419-7695-6_29
18. de Albuquerque Siebra, C., Botelho Neto, G.P.: Evolving the behavior of autonomous agents in strategic combat scenarios via sarsa reinforcement learning. In: Proceedings of the 2014 Brazilian Symposium on Computer Games and Digital Entertainment, SBGAMES 2014, Washington, DC, USA, pp. 115–122. IEEE Computer Society (2014). https://doi.org/10.1109/SBGAMES.2014.36
19. Šošić, A., KhudaBukhsh, W.R., Zoubir, A.M., Koeppl, H.: Inverse reinforcement learning in swarm systems. In: Proceedings of the 16th Conference on Autonomous Agents and MultiAgent Systems, pp. 1413–1421. International Foundation for Autonomous Agents and Multiagent Systems (2017)
20. Svetlik, M., Leonetti, M., Sinapov, J., Shah, R., Walker, N., Stone, P.: Automatic curriculum graph generation for reinforcement learning agents, November 2016. http://eprints.whiterose.ac.uk/108931/
21. Torrens, P.M., Nara, A., Li, X., Zhu, H., Griffin, W.A., Brown, S.B.: An extensible simulation environment and movement metrics for testing walking behavior in agent-based models. Comput. Environ. Urban Syst. **36**(1), 1–17 (2012)
22. Yamashita, T., Soeda, S., Noda, I.: Evacuation planning assist system with network model-based pedestrian simulator. In: Yang, J.-J., Yokoo, M., Ito, T., Jin, Z., Scerri, P. (eds.) PRIMA 2009. LNCS (LNAI), vol. 5925, pp. 649–656. Springer, Heidelberg (2009). https://doi.org/10.1007/978-3-642-11161-7_52
23. Zanlungo, F., Ikeda, T., Kanda, T.: Social force model with explicit collision prediction. EPL (Europhys. Lett.) **93**(6), 68005 (2011)
24. Zhong, J., Cai, W., Luo, L., Zhao, M.: Learning behavior patterns from video for agent-based crowd modeling and simulation. Auton. Agents Multi-Agent Syst. **30**(5), 990–1019 (2016)
25. Ziebart, B.D., Maas, A.L., Bagnell, J.A., Dey, A.K.: Maximum entropy inverse reinforcement learning. In: AAAI, Chicago, IL, USA, vol. 8, pp. 1433–1438 (2008)

FARM: Architecture for Distributed Agent-Based Social Simulations

Jim Blythe$^{(\boxtimes)}$ and Alexey Tregubov$^{(\boxtimes)}$

Information Sciences Institute, Marina del Rey, CA 90292, USA
blythe@isi.edu, tregubov@usc.edu

Abstract. In many domains, high-resolution agent-based simulations require experiments with a large number (tens or hundreds of millions) of computationally complex agents. Such large-scale experiments are usually run for efficiency on high-performance computers or clusters, and therefore agent-based simulation frameworks must support parallel distributed computations. The development of experiments with a large number of interconnected agents and a shared environment running in parallel on multiple compute nodes is especially challenging because it introduces the overhead of cross-process communications.

In this paper we discuss the parallel distributed architecture of the FARM agent-based simulation framework for social network simulations. To address the issue of shared environment synchronization we used a hybrid approach that distributes the simulation environment across compute nodes and keeps the shared portions of the environment synchronized via centralized memory storage. To minimize cross-process communication overhead, we allocate agents to processes via a graph partitioning algorithm that minimizes edge cuts in the communication graph, estimated in our domain by empirical data of past agent activities. The implementation of the toolkit used off the shelf components to support centralized storage and messaging/notification services.

This architecture was used in a large-scale Github simulation with up to ten million agents. In experiments in this domain, the graph partitioning algorithm cut overall runtime by 67% on average.

Keywords: Agent-based modeling and simulation ·
Parallel distributed simulation · Large-scale simulation ·
Parallel distributed computing

1 Introduction

The development of large-scale agent-based simulations for social science can require significant computational resources. In order to simulate social networks such as Facebook, Twitter or Github with high resolution, including models of individual users, one may need to simulate hundreds of millions of agents. Each agent may have a complex behaviour model that requires a significant amount of information from the environment. A large number of complex agents exchanging

© Springer Nature Switzerland AG 2019
D. Lin et al. (Eds.): MMAS 2018, LNAI 11422, pp. 96–107, 2019.
https://doi.org/10.1007/978-3-030-20937-7_7

information with the shared environment inevitably consumes a large amount of computational power.

The efficient simulation of large models often requires more computational resources than are available to the researcher on one machine. Therefore, it is often necessary to utilize resources of high performance super computers or clusters. Clusters require parallel computations. There are two main technical reasons to use clusters of computers and parallel computations: (1) to make simulations run faster and (2) to overcome the memory limitations of a single machine. Running an agent-based simulation on such platforms requires support of parallel computations in the architecture of the simulation framework. In this paper, we present FARM, a distributed parallel agent simulation architecture with centralized storage and messaging services. FARM's distributed architecture was designed to addresses parallel simulation challenges such as a synchronized shared environment and cross-process communication overhead. As part of its solution, FARM uses a combination of centralized and distributed storage. Centralized storage is used for portions of the environment that must be shared by agents on different compute nodes, and the local memory of a node is used in all other cases. Since communication between compute nodes (cross-process communication) uses the network, it significantly slows the overall simulation time. We discuss methods, including graph-based agent partitioning and smart lazy communication, to minimize cross-process communication to reduce simulation runtime and increase the size of simulations that can be run in practice.

FARM has been used to run simulations approaching 10 million agents on 10 nodes with 16 GB RAM, or on 4 nodes with 64 GB RAM, simulating 30 million events in approximately one hour of real time. The novel contributions of FARM include (1) explicit reasoning about centralized and distributed storage at run time and (2) graph-based partitioning of agents between compute nodes based on empirical communication data. FARM's distributed parallel architecture was utilized to overcome memory limitation of compute nodes at expense of cross-process communication overhead. The impact of cross-process communication overhead was reduced by optimized graph-based partitioning of agents between compute nodes.

We present empirical results from a simulation of millions of Github user agents on the performance of the partitioning algorithm. In our experiments, the algorithm cuts overall runtime by around 67% on average and cuts the amount of cross-process communication required by 70%. We conclude with a discussion of next steps to further improve performance at very large scale, enabling high-fidelity agent simulations to be applied to city-scale or nation-scale domains.

2   Related Work

Two types of parallel processing are described in the agent-based simulation literature: (1) simulations that run a large a number of experiment trials in parallel and (2) simulations that run one large computationally complex experiment trial in parallel on several compute nodes. Many distributed parallel agent-based simulations were originally developed using the first approach [3, 4, 10]. However, in such domains as transportation, where a large number of active agents is necessary in each experiment run, the resources of one computer are often not enough even for one trial of the experiment. For example, to simulate air traffic over the US models need to handle more than 40000 flights [12]. In such simulations, agents usually follow some simple rules to model physical interactions of the real world, and experiments often need hundreds of thousands of them.

The development of parallel distributed simulations, exploiting the power of parallel computation, has been used to approach scalability of multi-agent simulations [4]. In the distributed simulation models described in [5,11,12] agents are partitioned by geographical location where partitions allowed concurrent execution. When agents move due to their actions from one region to another they are reallocated to a process corresponding to a new region or partition of the environment. For example, Šišlák et al. [11] proposed an architecture for distributed parallel simulation of air traffic control using the locality of interactions among agents and the environment to distribute agents across several computers. General purpose agent-based simulation frameworks also heavily rely on the locality of agent interactions with their environments (e.g. the agent only partially observes the environment). For instance, in Repast the grid-locality of communications with the environment is a part of the framework for parallel simulations [4]. This principle of distributing agents across compute nodes according to their location and sphere of influence is common among agent-based simulations in social, economic and climate studies [6,10].

Compared with transportation or economic domains, simulations of social networks with high resolution may require an even larger number of agents. Social networks such as Facebook and Twitter have hundreds of millions of monthly active users. Additionally, communication among social network users is often not bounded by geographical location, and so partitioning agents and the environment in distributed parallel simulations also requires a different approach. In Github simulation experiments, discussed in the following sections, we applied graph-based partitioning of agents between compute nodes based on empirical communication data.

3 FARM Distributed Simulation Architecture

FARM supports distributing agent simulations across multiple compute hosts in parallel to enable large-scale multi-agent simulations. It supports two cases of distributed processing for multi-agent simulations: one case in which a single simulation is distributed across multiple compute nodes, and one in which an experiment consists of many repeated trials, each a separate simulation, which are distributed across multiple compute nodes. Each compute node is an independent process running on its own host. FARM includes support for explicitly representing experiments consisting of multiple trials, iterating over the set of independent variables, in support of a hypothesis. However, in this paper we focus on support for a single simulation distributed across multiple hosts, since the trials within an experiment are independent of each other, and hence simpler to allocate from a computational standpoint.

FARM is implemented in Python and designed to support simulations involving DASH agents. DASH is a platform for developing cognitive agents, also written in Python [2]. During a simulation, DASH agents can either affect each other directly, through peer-to-peer communication, or indirectly through one altering some part of the shared state that the other perceives. This indirect communication is moderated through a DASH communication hub, that receives information from agents about actions that were taken and passes back the observable results of the action, while modeling the world state within the simulation. However, FARM can be used with simulations involving other kinds of agent representations.

We assume that each compute host will run many agents within the simulation in a single image, with inter-agent communication between agents on the same compute host supported efficiently by shared memory within the image. FARM utilizes centralized storage and messaging service to synchronize the environment that agents share in simulation. FARM provides tools for automated management of simulation parameters and allows the researcher to control experiment setup.

Figure 1 shows the distributed architecture of FARM and how its components are allocated across multiple compute nodes. Each compute node runs a process, called DASH Worker, that runs a subset of agents and maintains a synchronized view of the part of the simulation environment that must be shared between nodes.

On each DASH Worker, the part of the state that is used by only agents on that DASH Worker is kept locally, while the rest is shared, and maintained via an in-memory database. Information about the state updates is distributed via messaging services. FARM uses Apache ZooKeeper [1] to provide a fast in-memory database for small transactions and messaging/notification services for task distribution and synchronization.

FARM uses the DASH agent-based simulation framework, where DASH agents communicate with each other and interact with their shared environment via communication hubs. DASH communication hubs accept action specifications from agents and return their observable effects, while maintaining the shared state of the environment as a result of these actions. Each compute node has at least one communication hub. Communication hubs synchronize their portion of the environment with other hubs in the network as needed via Apache ZooKeeper.

Typically the environment represents some shared resources of the simulation (e.g. posts, pages, pictures on social networks, source code repositories on Github, etc.). FARM distributes agents and environment resources (via communication hubs) across multiple compute nodes. Communication between agents and shared resources of the environment can therefore be viewed as an agent-to-resource graph. For example, in the Github experiment, discussed below, the shared environment consists of software repositories that agents observe and contribute to, and the agent-to-resource graph is then a user-to-repository communication graph (labeled as U-R graph in figures). This is a bipartite graph

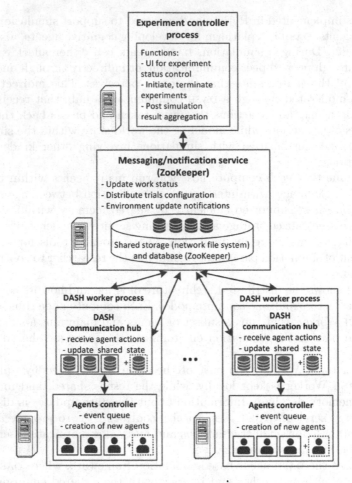

Fig. 1. The FARM distributed simulation architecture.

of agents and shared resources; two vertices in the graph are connected when agents access the shared tresource. Frequencies of interaction between agents and shared resources can be used as weights in the graph.

The agent-to-resource graph is partitioned when agents are allocated to compute nodes. Cross-process communication in the simulation then corresponds to the case where two agents allocated to different compute nodes access the same resource. If information about expected agent communication is available, it can be used to partition an agent-to-resource graph in a way that reduces this cross-process communication during simulations. Past communication history between agents and the environment can be used to build an agent-to-resource graph. Graph partitioning algorithms that reduce the total flow across edge cuts can then be used to partition the agent-to-resource graph and find an efficient allocation of agents to compute nodes.

In FARM we utilized a k-way graph partitioning algorithms implemented in METIS [8,9]. METIS uses multilevel partitioning algorithms that reduce the size of the graph by collapsing vertices and edges, partition the smaller graph, and then uncoarsen it to construct a partition for the original graph. METIS utilizes novel algorithms developed by Karypis and Kumar [8,9]. These algorithms allow parallel work on large graphs as well as multi-constraint partitioning.

4 Github Simulation and Experiment Setup

In this section we discuss a Github simulation model (shown in Fig. 2), which was implemented using the distributed architecture presented above. Github [7] is a hosting platform for software repositories using the git version control software, that provides additional features such as wikis. Github is an example of a social network where users can comment on commits, make pull requests, fork repositories, create branches, etc. There are several dozens of millions of users and repositories on Github. Our Github simulation is capable of running several million agents and repositories simultaneously on multiple compute nodes.

The DASH architecture provides the necessary components to model social networks. In our Github experiment, DASH agents represent Github users, and DASH communication hubs model the social network infrastructure. Communication hubs provide access to a shared state of the environment—the Github repositories. The state of repositories reflect the history of other users' actions on a particular repository, and it can drive next actions of an agent. For example, if one user submits a pull request, another user may respond to that request by accepting or rejecting it.

The goal of the Github experiment was to simulate interactions between agents and repositories. This also allowed us to test the performance of the simulation framework in different configurations—using different agent partitioning techniques and different number of compute nodes in different trials.

We measured the overall simulation runtime and the number of cross-process communications, which is the number of times compute nodes synchronized the state of their repositories.

In this experiment an agent-to-resource graph is called user-to-repository graph. To compare the quality of an user-to-repository graph partitioning techniques, we measured the number of edge cuts in the partitioned graph. The number of graph partitions is the same as the number of compute nodes in this experiment.

We compared two partitioning algorithms: random user-to-node allocation and multilevel k-way graph partitioning using the METIS library [8,9]. In random user-to-node allocation, the number of users per node was balanced, and all repositories that are only accessed by one user were allocated to the same node as the user. This means that only repositories that are accessed by two or more users could belong to edge cuts.

We used all user activities on Github for one month as a training dataset, modeling the actions taken such as forking a repository or committing code,

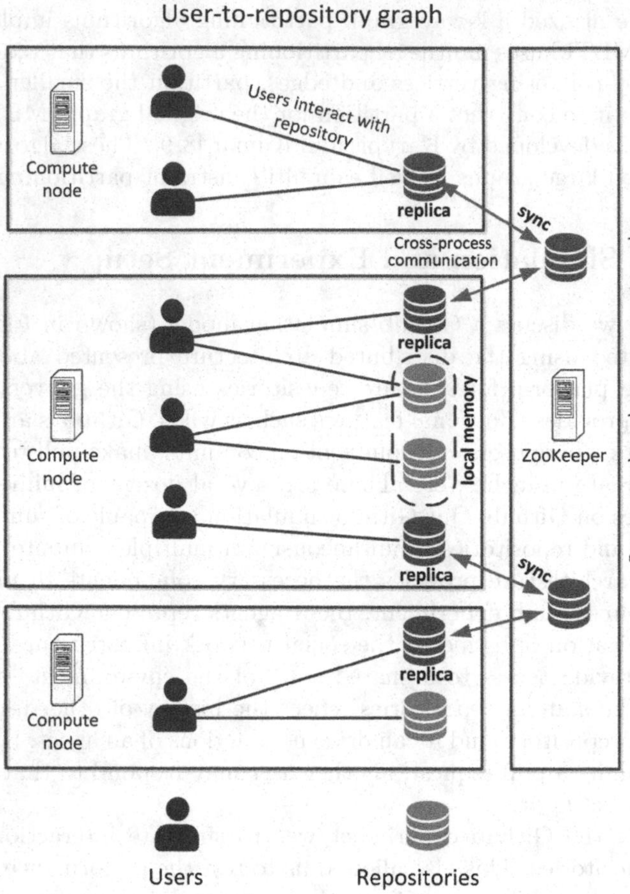

User-to-repository graph

Fig. 2. The distributed Github simulation allocates each agent to a single compute node. Repositories are modeled locally if they affect only agents from one compute node, otherwise they are replicated.

but not storing the content of the code that was committed. This provided the initial state of the simulation with 1.8 million users and 3.2 million repositories. We chose this size of the initial state as a realistic representation of the scale required to model active users and repositories on Github over a reasonable time period. The simulation ran on a cluster of 18 compute nodes, each with 16 GB of RAM and 4 core CPUs. However, in order to measure cross-process communication overhead in multiple trials, we designed a reduced model with simplified agents so that the entire simulation could fit into 16 GB of RAM on one compute node. These simplified agents did not use the cognitive modeling capabilities that are available in DASH and had a relatively restricted memory of their history of Github activity.

We also ran trials in which the state of the repositories shared between partitions was not synchronized (labeled as 'no sync') to measure results without the cross-process communication overhead. These simulations were, of course, incorrect, but they enabled us to measure task allocation and aggregation separately from the cross-process repository communication.

5   Results

Figure 3 shows simulation runtime of all 36 trials. In most of the trials, METIS user-to-repository graph partitioning ran more than three times faster than random partitioning. METIS user-to-repository graph partitioning algorithm allowed 3% load imbalance and was configured to minimize the number of edge cuts. It is important to note that minimizing edge cuts in user-to-repository graph is an approximation to minimizing the number of repositories shared between several partitions.

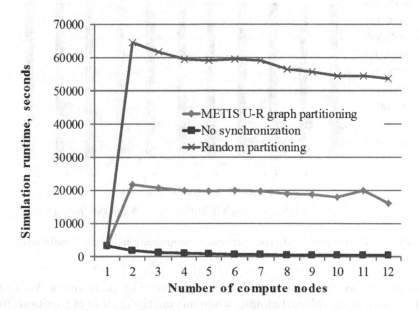

Fig. 3. Simulation runtime with different partitioning algorithms. In order to test results with fewer nodes, simplified agents have been used that can fit in 16 GB of RAM on a single machine. In more faithful experiments, a cluster of 18 nodes was used.

Runtime decreases with the number of available computation nodes. However, due to cross-process communication overhead, the runtime of trials with several compute nodes is always significantly higher (10–20 times) than the runtime of a trial running one just one node. In general, it is not always feasible to fit the whole simulation model and all its agents in one compute node. More complex agent behavior requires more computational time and memory, which may not be available on one machine.

Figure 4 shows the number of cross-process communications in trials with a varying number of compute nodes. We can see that cross-process communication with random partitioning increases only by 5% when the number of compute nodes goes from 2 to 12 nodes. For METIS k-way graph partitioning it increases by 48%, and it remains mostly the same when more than 9 nodes used. This means that after some number of nodes the number of cross-process communications does not increase.

On average, in our domain, cross-process communications constituted 31% of user to repository interaction under a random user allocation, and 9% under user allocation that used METIS k-way graph partitioning.

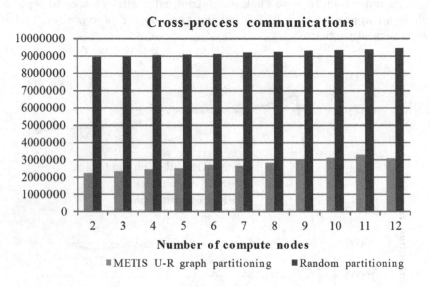

Fig. 4. Total number of cross-process communications in the simulation.

Figure 5 shows the number of edge cuts produced by partitioning. We tested user-to-repository graph partitioning while varying the number of partitions from 2 to 18. Random partitioning produces almost the same number of edge cuts regardless of the number of partitions, whereas for METIS k-way graph partitioning, the number of edge cuts levels off after 10 partitions. In all cases, the METIS k-way graph partitioning produces at least three times fewer edge cuts. This is consistent with the runtime, since the number of edge cuts directly impacts the amount of cross-process communication and runtime.

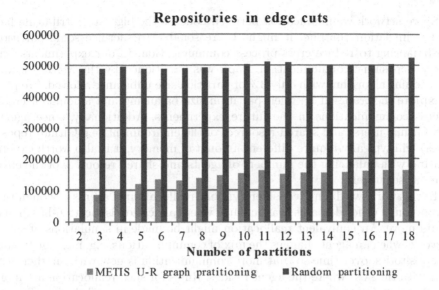

Fig. 5. Total number of repositories that belongs to more than one partition (edge cuts). METIS multilevel k-way graph partitioning and random partitioning.

6   Discussion

One of the main difficulties of distributed parallel simulations is maintaining shared state synchronization, which requires cross-process communication. The amount of cross-process communication significantly slows down the overall simulation runtime. Partitioning of the agent communication graph can significantly reduce the amount of cross-process communications and runtime.

In this research we conducted experiments using the distributed FARM architecture with a hybrid of centralized and distributed storage for shared state synchronization. We measured performance of different agent-to-node allocation strategies. In our Github simulation experiment, the METIS multilevel k-way graph partitioning reduced the number of cross-process communications and runtime more than three times compare to a balanced random agent-to-node allocation.

This distributed architecture is applicable for different domains. In the Github experiment we used the history of user-repository interactions to allocate agents to compute nodes. Different domains might use different agent partitioning techniques, for example, the geographical location of agents. If the simulation model allows identifying highly interconnected clusters of agents that mostly share only some small portion of the environment (e.g. in Github experiment it is a group of users that mostly only work their own repositories), then the hybrid storage architecture of DASH can take advantage of this to reduce cross-process communications and runtime.

Since network communication between nodes is the biggest contributing factor to simulation runtime, it might be reasonable to sacrifice some partition size balancing to reduce cross-process communication. In our experiments, the user-to-repository communication graph was partitioned by the METIS k-way partitioning algorithm with only 3% of partition size imbalance allowed. We plan to explore the trade-off between partition size balancing and amount of cross-process communications in the future experiments. Additionally, since agents (e.g. Github users) and shared resources of the environment (e.g Github repositories) will typically require different amount of memory, it is also worth experimenting with balancing the numbers of agents and shared resources of the environment separately.

In this work, we did not consider dynamic reallocation of agents although this is common in other domains, particularly where allocation is location-based and agents move. An equivalent reallocation might be made in simulations of social networks when an agent changes the mix of communications, e.g. message boards or repositories, over time so that more communication is now with another host than with the host where the agent resides. Rules for such reallocation are more complex than in the case of location-based agents, however, and the benefits not always as clear.

There are benefits and limitations to the centralized storage architecture that we have discussed. Compared to fully distributed peer-to-peer communication the centralized storage and messaging service are conceptually easier to use and maintain when a distributed simulation model is being developed. Additionally, there are many off-the-shelf components available to make the implementation efficient. Large-scale simulations also require a very high throughput from the database and messaging service, which can make them a bottleneck. Apache ZooKeeper allows distributed installations and also supports local caching and delayed/lazy synchronization transparent for the simulation model, which can be used to fine-tune the simulation performance.

In large-scale simulations with several million agents running on multiple nodes, it is likely to find clusters of agents that share a similar or identical internal state. In such cases, it may be possible to compress the representation of the internal state of these agents to make the simulation more memory efficient. This in turn allows more agents to be allocated to the same node, which can reduce the total number of compute nodes and cross-process communications. We are currently exploring performance optimization such as these in FARM.

Acknowledgment. This material is based upon work supported by the Defense Advanced Research Projects Agency (DARPA) and the Army Research Office (ARO) under Contract No. W911NF-17-C-0094. Any opinions, findings and conclusions or recommendations expressed in this material are those of the author(s) and do not necessarily reflect the views of the Defense Advanced Research Projects Agency (DARPA) and the Army Research Office (ARO).

References

1. Apache: Apache zookeeper (2018). https://zookeeper.apache.org
2. Blythe, J.: A dual-process cognitive model for testing resilient control systems. In: 5th International Symposium on Resilient Control Systems, pp. 8–12, August 2012
3. Chow, K.P., Kwok, Y.K.: On load balancing for distributed multiagent computing. IEEE Trans. Parallel Distrib. Syst. **13**(8), 787–801 (2002)
4. Collier, N., North, M.: Parallel agent-based simulation with repast for high performance computing. Simulation **89**(10), 1215–1235 (2013)
5. Cosenza, B., Cordasco, G., De Chiara, R., Scarano, V.: Distributed load balancing for parallel agent-based simulations. In: 2011 19th Euromicro International Conference on Parallel, Distributed and Network-Based Processing (PDP), pp. 62–69. IEEE (2011)
6. Deissenberg, C., Van Der Hoog, S., Dawid, H.: EURACE: a massively parallel agent-based model of the european economy. Appl. Math. Comput. **204**(2), 541–552 (2008)
7. Github: Github software development platform (2018). http://github.com
8. Karypis, G., Kumar, V.: Multilevel algorithms for multi-constraint graph partitioning. In: Proceedings of the 1998 ACM/IEEE Conference on Supercomputing, pp. 1–13. IEEE Computer Society (1998)
9. Karypis, G., Kumar, V.: Multilevelk-way partitioning scheme for irregular graphs. J. Parallel Distrib. Comput. **48**(1), 96–129 (1998)
10. Scheutz, M., Schermerhorn, P., Connaughton, R., Dingler, A.: SWAGES-an extendable distributed experimentation system for large-scale agent-based alife simulations. In: Proceedings of Artificial Life X, pp. 412–419 (2006)
11. Šišlák, D., Volf, P., Jakob, M., Pěchouček, M.: Distributed platform for large-scale agent-based simulations. In: Dignum, F., Bradshaw, J., Silverman, B., van Doesburg, W. (eds.) AGS 2009. LNCS (LNAI), vol. 5920, pp. 16–32. Springer, Heidelberg (2009). https://doi.org/10.1007/978-3-642-11198-3_2
12. Tumer, K., Agogino, A.: Distributed agent-based air traffic flow management. In: Proceedings of the 6th International Joint Conference on Autonomous Agents and Multiagent Systems, AAMAS 2007, pp. 255:1–255:8. ACM, New York (2007). https://doi.org/10.1145/1329125.1329434

Applications of Massively Multi-agent Systems

Diversity in Massively Multi-agent Systems: Concepts, Implementations, and Normal Accidents

Philip Feldman[1,3] and Antonio Bucchiarone[2(✉)]

[1] University of Maryland, Baltimore County, MD, USA
[2] Fondazione Bruno Kessler, Trento, Italy
bucchiarone@fbk.eu
[3] ASRC Federal, Laurel, MD, USA

Abstract. Coordination for Transportation as a Service (TaaS) can be implemented on a spectrum, ranging from independent agents communicating exclusively through market exchanges to hybrid market/hierarchy approaches fixed hierarchical control systems. An overview of each approach is described and a detailed description of recent work in simulating a hybrid solution is presented. The use of diversity as a potential approach to reduce the impact of catastrophic Normal Accidents is discussed.

Keywords: Diversity · Multi-agent systems ·
Transportation as a Service · Market systems · Hierarchical control ·
Distributed control

1 Introduction

Through most of history, the allocation of transportation resources has not been an issue. The trouble arose once we started to ride horses, sail boats, ride trains and travel in cars. Transportation resources can be expensive. In 2016, the average US consumer spent $8,427 on vehicles [2], or approximately 20% of the median US household income of $43,290 for that year [3]. Clearly, using transportation services more efficiently can create enormous savings for the individual, while simultaneously reducing congestion and pollution in areas where these efficiencies are achieved.

Transportation as a Service (TaaS) is the application of information technology to the movement of people at the individual level. Scheduling and allocation that was previously only cost effective for transportation of users as groups can now be allocated down to the level of an internet-connected, GPS equipped bicycle or e-scooter. Fifteen years ago, the integration of internet-connected, GPS equipped trucks disrupted the trucking industry, allowing for the emergence of markets that allowed individual owner-operators to bid competitively across a number of freight exchanges [5].

But people are different from cargo. They have agency, and the cost of even relatively minor errors can be high. They also have requirements that cargo

D. Lin et al. (Eds.): MMAS 2018, LNAI 11422, pp. 111–129, 2019.
https://doi.org/10.1007/978-3-030-20937-7_8

doesn't, like cognitive load and status. How can these transportation needs be efficiently met? In this paper, we introduce TaaS as a *massively multi-agent system* able to cover a diverse technological spectrum ranging from tightly structured hierarchies to open markets. We then describe in detail research into a middle ground consisting of loosely connected ensembles of hierarchies. Lastly, we discuss some of the implications that can arise from building densely connected, highly responsive transportation networks, particularly with respect to unanticipated, extreme conditions.

2   The TaaS Spectrum of Coordination

Optimizing transportation isn't just hard, it's *NP-Hard*. As seen with just a single traveling salesman, the number of paths scales geometrically with the number of towns to visit. Even such apparently simple transport problems such as determining the staging and stops for a set of elevators in a skyscraper remain unsolved, and have recently been analyzed using machine learning techniques [14]. With distributed systems supporting potentially billions of people utilizing millions of devices, a closed form solution is clearly impossible. Rather, we need to focus on attainable benchmarks to evaluate potential and actual systems.

Wellman, in his work on market-oriented programming [35] suggests the following criteria for evaluating distributed systems:

- What is the quality of the allocation of resources?
- How computationally intensive is the allocation process?
- How easy is it to design and specify a system?

Since these criteria were developed in 1994, large scale wireless networks have become a daily reality along with hacking and security breaches. As such, we suggest adding the following criteria:

- How much bandwidth is needed? Particularly in situations where communication can be unreliable, the speed and number of bytes needed to achieve a complete transaction needs to be considered.
- How resilient is the system to unforeseen conditions? Can the system adapt rapidly and effectively to conditions that significantly disrupt normal transportation patterns, such as evacuations, natural disasters and even wars?
- How secure is the system? Is the system vulnerable as a whole or parts? Can the system be hacked to the point that a vehicle becomes a danger to its passengers and others?

With these criteria in mind, we now look to the three main regions that define this spectrum - market-based, hybrid, and hierarchical.

2.1   Market Systems

The Oxford English Dictionary defines "stock exchange" as A market for the buying and selling of public securities; the place or building where this is done; an association of brokers and jobbers who transact business in a particular place or market [1].

Although we could find no online exchanges for TaaS for people, there are online transportation exchanges for cargo have been in existence for about 20 years, and three particular categories have emerged; clearing houses, auctions, and freight exchanges [25].

Clearing houses collect the loads posted by the shippers or capacity posted by carriers. Both parties search for their preferred choice and negotiate one-on-one for the price of delivery. Lyft, Uber and other transportation network companies (TNCs) tend to incorporate a private version of this model as private clearing houses for matching user requests and ride providers.

Auction houses engage both carriers and shippers to sell their capacity or delivery services at the best price. The auction system has been found to improve their occupancy rate of transport vehicles while shippers can obtain better rates under spot market circumstances.

Freight exchanges let shippers post their demands and carriers posts their capacity in an online marketplace where each of them will be allocated to their respective services required at a competitive price.

Market systems are generally regarded to be an extremely efficient way to allocate resources. Agent-based simulation [33] shows that transportation markets can achieve Pareto equilibrium, where no user can improve their position without making another agent's position worse. Markets can be gamed however. For example, in eBay auctions users tend to pile on bids an the last few seconds of an auction in a process called sniping. This tends to force a lower price, benefiting the bidder.

The amount of computation scales geometrically with the number of users and providers. Multiple heuristics can be applied to the data to reduce the amount of computation. For example, riders and providers that are near enough to each other need be evaluated. That being said, in dense urban environments, that could still be a computationally intensive task, where "good enough" answers would have to be accepted.

Since private clearing houses for TaaS have been deployed, it is clear that such systems can be built and deployed at scale. Lyft and Uber both offer APIs for external developers to integrate other products into their respective corporate ecosystems. This is only front end interaction though. The full stack that performs global scale interactions clearly depends on hundreds of developers.

Bandwidth for market systems does not need to be large. At a minimum there needs to be a request by the consumer and a response by the provider. Additional, market-specific information such as time remaining on an auction adds very little data to a given payload. No real-time communication is *required* for the market, though meeting particular deadlines can be critical. Where bandwidth permits, companies often provide UIs where real-time information like vehicle location to the user.

Security in regulated exchanges such as the New York Stock Exchange seems surprisingly effective, even though glitches such as Flash Crashes occur [20]. One reason is that these systems are often on their own networks, and have circuit breakers that halt all trading. Also, each transaction is directly associated with a registered user who is financially liable for all transactions. This fiscal obligation has resulted in massive losses due to software glitches [13], so there is considerable motivation on the part of traders to self-police.

Markets can adapt quickly to changing conditions as long as the basic framework of the market remains intact. A power failure at a server farm could shut down a centralized exchange. Another issue is the fundamental nature of a market, where prices fluctuate, based on supply and demand. In the case of an evacuation order, a market-based TaaS could easily favor the rich as the price for transportation rises inversely with respect to supply. An example of this is surge pricing, which raises the cost of a ride at times of high demand. A market can't adjust organically to such issues, so specific policies have to be put in place. For example, Uber put a cap on fares during the evacuation of sections of Florida prior to the landfall of hurricane Irma [22].

Research Challenges. As stated in the previous section, a private, central exchange is vulnerable to a sufficiently widespread catastrophe. Distributed, public exchanges could address this weakness, but building distributed trustworthy systems is difficult. Yuan and Wang develop a blockchain-based mechanism for intelligent transportation services [37], but there are high computation costs associated with creating ledgers. Furthermore, blockchain requires all transacting computers to be connected. An orphan network, such as might occur during a catastrophe would have to halt transactions. Other, tangle-based systems could be more resilient, and support isolated networks [28]. This would be important research, because a system that could support isolated markets could support any technology that can interact with the exchange, for example, the use of horses could emerge in the case of chronic fuel shortages.

2.2   Hierarchical Control Systems

Hierarchical control predates digital embodiments, with examples as diverse as companies, armies, and governments. As such, it is an intuitive concept for control systems that was described in considerable detail by Roth, in 1962 [30]. In his article, Roth describes the major components, communication requirements, separation of responsibility, and human integration that are still the basis for today's systems.

The National Institute of Standards and Technology has implemented a framework for large scale real-time control, the *NIST Real-time Control (RCS) Reference Model Architecture* [29]. NIST formalized RCS as a standard reference architecture and implemented this framework across multiple domains, ranging from vehicle control to robot control to manufacturing.

RCS is based on the concept of hierarchical task decomposition. A complicated task, such as painting a car, can be broken down along levels of abstraction.

At the highest level is the overall command paint the next car red. This command is then broken down into commands that are issued to the subcomponents, such as the painting robot and the auto body transport elements. At the lowest levels of abstraction the servos that move the various actuators are controlled. At the lowest levels of the system, updates rates are thousands of times a second. At the highest levels updates need only occur every few minutes.

The logic to perform a task is contained in an RCS *Controller Module*. All controllers have the same structure:

1. A command buffer, which contains the command (e.g. MOVE_TO_START), and a serial number.
2. A response buffer which contains an echo of the command, a status (e.g. WORKING, DONE, ERROR) and a serial number.
3. A set of command and response buffers for any child controllers.
4. A window to world data, that contains environmental information. Sensors controlled modules that could be useful to other modules are published here.
5. A preprocess that reads in any parent commands, child responses, and environmental data.
6. A decision process, that takes the command and the current state of the controller and decides what task is active.
7. A collection of finite state machines that perform the amount of the task within the update rate.
8. A postprocess where responses to the parent, commands to the children, and any useful sensor data is published.

Modules are connected in a strict hierarchy - no module may have two parents. Because each command has a serial number that is echoed back in the response, all direct interaction between modules is deterministic, and can tolerate poor communication - a command can't be sent until the response echoes back the serial number. RCS can also be used in simulations. The controllers interact with a physics based environment that provides enough information for the sensors and actuators to behave within reasonable parameters. Because controllers contain all process knowledge related to a task at their level of abstraction, communication between controllers is typically minimal. This in turn affords easy modification and adjustment of the hierarchy, so as a task or technology changes, only small parts of the running system need to be modified.

Hierarchies do not allocate resources well. The top-down nature of the control stands in opposition to the bottom-up self organization of market systems. What this means is that the allocation scheme has to be encoded in the structure of the particular control hierarchy. When this is done, and for those explicit instances, allocation can be extremely rapid and efficient. The moment the problem envelope exceeds the ability of the hierarchy to accommodate it, the control hierarchy can no longer adapt.

Control hierarchies can be designed to be optimally efficient, since the entire structure is known. Further, each component is trusted, additional work to determine trustworthiness (e.g. Blockchain calculations) is not needed. Short of a monolithic system, a control hierarchy should be able to embody the lowest computational intensity for well-defined tasks.

NIST RCS in particular is designed specifically to reduce cognitive load. Controllers handle a single task, using the same *preprocess/decision process/state table/post process* pattern. Developers quickly learn this methodology and can easily contribute to developers working on different controllers. Debugging tools that monitor the commands and responses between controllers provide high level views of the functioning of the overall system, while drilldown into the common state table operations within each controller can also be visualized using tools that understand the RCS implementation.

A properly designed hierarchy has very low bandwidth requirements due to the compartmentalization of the tasks within controllers. In places like high-speed servo control, where multiple child controllers may need to react to rapid commands by a parent controller, the system can be designed such that all hardware shares a high-speed communication channel.

Because they are designed to deal with a particular environment, a factory floor, a submarine, an autonomous vehicle, hierarchical control systems do not have an inherent capacity to adapt to a different control environment. If new hardware replaces old hardware on the factory floor, the control system must be adjusted too. A good hierarchy makes this easy to do, with minimum impact on the rest of the running system, but that is different from expecting the hierarchy to adapt to the new hardware.

Due to the explicit design of the system and the reuse of common components such as controllers, it is possible to design and build an extremely secure control hierarchy. That being said, if the top level controller is hacked, the rest of the system will blindly follow. As a rule, the risks of broken security lessen as the control system moves away from the hierarchical side of the spectrum.

Research Challenges. A great deal of research has been performed on adaptive hierarchical control systems [19, 32]. Hierarchical systems have inherent disadvantages in that they need complete information across sub-systems to coordinate control down to the individual actuators. As such, a designer of a large scale, low response time system (such as a nuclear reactor) has to be aware of all possible interactions within the system, since an actuator far down a one branch of software involved with emergency response may vent high-pressure radioactive steam into a section of plumbing normally involved with the steam used for powering turbines [27]. The issue here is one of the combinatorial explosion of possibilities that can occur in monolithic systems. Working though all potential combinations is possible on small systems, but rapidly becomes uncomputable as the hierarchy grows.

If, on the other hand, small, testable hierarchies can be linked so that rapid response and control happens within the hierarchy, but looser interactions can exist *between hierarchies* then more resilient systems can be designed. These sets of smaller hierarchies can operate in clusters or ensembles could have the ability to operate using local information and respond in more adaptive, flexible ways to a scoped set of problems. This approach is discussed in the next section, where we use urban mobility to explore how adaptive ensembles of hierarchies can blend market flexibility and hierarchical control.

3   Ensembles of Hierarchies

Modern cities are complex socio-technical entities that exist to provide services effectively to their residents and visitors. Networks for water, electricity, communications, and finance permeate the urban environment. Further, people need to travel quickly and conveniently between locations at different scales, ranging from a trip of a few blocks to a journey across town or further. Each trip has its set of requirements. Time may be of the essence. Cost may be paramount and the convenience of door-to-door travel may be important. In each case, the transportation infrastructure should seamlessly provide the best option. A modern city needs to flexibly integrate transportation options including buses, trains, taxis, bicycles and cars. The combinatorial complexity of all these possibilities negates the option of a single, monolithic control system. How would a grouping, or ensemble of hierarchies perform in this situation?

In this section, we consider a simplified urban mobility system (UMS), that comprises several means of transportation that are collectively managed. We focus on the aspect of adaptivity in situations where computational agents and affected human (e.g passengers, drivers) collectively reach adaptation decisions. In the following we describe the scenario and demonstrate the challenges it poses to collectively adapting socio-technical systems like UMS.

Our UMS consists of the following means of transportation:

- *Regular bus* service, a network of fixed bus routes with fixed timetable;
- *Flexible Bus (FB)*, a service that collects trip requests from customers and organizes on-demand routes that efficiently serve the requests;
- *Car Pool*, a service to share car journeys so that more than one person travels in a car;
- *Taxi*, a conventional taxi service;

Each means of transportation has a complex internal substructure. For example the FB service allows third party minibus owners to register their availability for serving trips, and for customers to register trip requests (e.g., location, time). The service dynamically creates routes on the basis of time and location of the trips requested and the availability of vehicles. Each FB route is an unit comprised of the vehicle (or FB driver) that is supposed to serve the route, and passengers traveling within similar time and location spans. A FB route is supervised by the FB company that provides all necessary infrastructure. It is easy to see that a FB route is a good example of collaborative behavior: passengers sacrifice part of their flexibility in order to travel cheaper, compared to a taxi, and quicker compared to conventional buses.

As shown in Fig. 1, our simulation of this system connects transportation with a set of agents that can interact in different ways. Agents can be part of several possible ensembles (i.e., from E1 to E9) according to their needs. Figure 1 shows the topology of the UMS example. It includes a hierarchical pattern but also direct relations, as in the Ensemble E9 composed by the FlexiBus Company (FBC) and the Car Pool Company (CPC).

To illustrate this, let us consider a messy but not unlikely scenario: A passenger is late for her FB, so the bus waits until she arrives. A current passenger, fed up by the extra waiting, leaves the bus to walk the remaining distance. To make up time the driver speeds and is involved in an accident, blocking traffic and requiring the FB company to rout around the congestion. This is not only a bad day for the passengers, it is an extremely complicated and expensive problem for the FB company. Its options include, among others:

1. refund passengers who cannot reach their destinations in time
2. reroute the running buses to prioritize the most affected customers
3. reroute the running buses so that the largest number of passengers reach their destinations on time
4. reassign passengers to other routes
5. reassign (groups of) passengers to other means of transportation

In the following subsection we analyze the challenges posed by this UMS scenario.

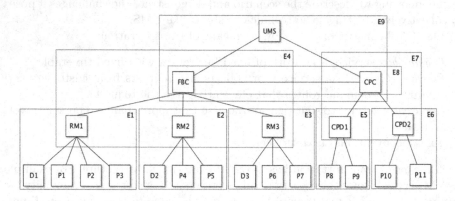

Fig. 1. Types of agents and ensembles in the UMS.

3.1   Research Challenges

The principal agents in the UMS scenario (i.e., passengers, FB drivers, FB company, etc.) are generally autonomous and act independently. This makes the system highly dynamic and distributed. The surrounding environment of an agent changes frequently and unpredictably (e.g. as other agents change their minds) and therefore the system requires constant monitoring and adaptation.

Existing approaches [34,36,39], normally deal with multi-agent adaptive systems through isolated adaptation: each agent adapts itself independently from each other. However, in our scenario the problem is complicated by collective behavior. Even though agents are generally autonomous, they dynamically form collaborative groups, called *ensembles*, to gain benefits that otherwise would not be possible. The example of such an ensemble is a FB route (E1 in Fig. 1) which coordinates the adaptation behavior of multiple agents (FB driver, passengers, and FB company) and in return gives them certain benefits (e.g., cheap and fast transportation). Membership of an ensemble may temporarily reduce the flexibility of its agents. Within this context, isolated agent self-adaptation is not effective. We can easily imagine what happens if a passenger books a trip with a FB and then silently changes their mind and decide not to travel. It is likely to cause unnecessary delay for the route (e.g. the bus will have a redundant stop) and raise the cost of the trip for the remaining passengers, including potential charges for the canceling passenger.

Even more serious consequences arise if a bus gets damaged: isolated adaptation by the bus driver could totally break the passengers' travel plans. Adaptation has to take into account not only customers trip requests but also customers constraints and preferences. For example, a particular passenger may want to avoid traveling through unsafe areas in the city, but a possible re-planned route may pass through such area.

The term *ensemble* has recently been introduced in the literature to denote very large-scale systems of systems that may present substantial socio-technical embedding [17,38]. They typify systems with complex design, engineering and management, whose level of complexity comes specifically from bringing together and combining in the same operating environment many heterogeneous and autonomous components, systems and users, with their specific concerns. To be robust against the high degree of unpredictability and dynamism of their operating environments, and to sustain the continuous variations induced by their socio-technical nature, ensembles need to self-adapt.

In adaptive systems with collective behavior, new approaches for adaptation are therefore needed that allow (i) multiple agents to collectively adapt with (ii) negotiations to decide which collective changes are best.

Collective adaptation also raises a second important challenge: *which parts of the system should be engaged in an adaptation?* This is not at all trivial, since solutions for the same problem may be generated at different levels. For instance, a passenger's delay may be resolved in the scope of a FB route, by re-planning the route, or in the wider scope of the FB company, with the engagement of other routes, or even in the scope of the whole UMS, with the engagement of other means of transportation such as a car pool. The challenge here is to understand these levels, formalize them and create a mechanism that decides the right scope for an adaptation for a given problem.

Within our scenario, we can identify several levels of abstraction that operate at different scales in time and space. An FB route combines passengers with a driver, a Flexibus company combines FB routes, and an UMS combines a

Flexibus company and other means of transportation. The higher the level of abstraction, the wider the scope of adaptation.

The *continuous and distributed adaptation* is a key feature of Collective Adaptive Systems (CAS), when it comes to operating in constantly changing environment. Concepts that are close to those introduced above, and that characterize CAS, have been studied in various domains such as, *Swarm Intelligence*, where actors are essentially homogeneous and are able to adapt their behavior considering only local knowledge [11,21], or *Autonomic computing*, where the actor types are typically limited and the adaptation is guided by predefined policies with the objective to optimize the system rather than evolve it [4], or *Service-based systems* where services are designed independently by different service providers and are composed to achieve a predefined goal (i.e., user tasks [6] or business goals [23]), or *Multi-agent based systems* where activities of different actors are regulated by certain collectively defined rules (i.e., norms) [12]. Most of the results obtained in these domains are tailored to solve a specific problem using a specific language or model and *lack of generality*.

At the same time, these studies tackle only some of the challenges for individual agents, while leaving decision-making for group, collective, and larger scales relatively unexamined.

For these reasons, we should move from *individual based applications* to *collective systems* with techniques that support adaptation of collectives. This will be achieved by defining *new software engineering methods* (i.e., models, theories and tools) that are highly flexible and can be specialized to fulfill different tasks in different ways. At the same time, they will introduce features for the collaboration and coordination among agents, as this is an essential prerequisite for building *collective adaptive systems (CAS)*. The collective nature of software systems, with the important aspect of the *diversity* that different agents bring in, makes the theme issue completely new and different with respect to previous issues in the field of engineering complex and adaptive systems. Models for CAS need to be *adaptable by design*; this means that each agent in the system must be able to adapt its behavior taking into account the current context/situation. The model should be flexible and extensible, fusing a priori and learned knowledge. The local knowledge of an agent should be extendable during its lifetime, based on collaboration with other agents and the current context of the adaptation. Finally, the model should consider the *heterogeneity* and *diversity* of the agents, incorporating the specific roles that they play in the collective.

In the next sections we introduce our approach that addresses the challenges above in order to facilitate collective adaptation.

3.2 General Framework

Our approach addresses the challenge of collective adaptation by proposing a new notion of ensembles that enables systems with collective adaptability to be built as emergent aggregations of autonomous and self-adaptive agents. Key properties of our approach include (i) the emphasis on collaboration towards fulfillment of individual, diverse goals, and (ii) the heterogeneous nature of an ensemble with respect to roles, behaviors and goals of its participants. These properties distinguish our approach from other types of ensemble models, like for instance swarms, where all elements of a community have a uniform behavior and global shared goal [11,21], and multi-agent systems and agent-based organizations [16], where there may be several distinct roles and behaviors, but the differentiation is still limited and often pre-designed.

We define an ensemble in terms of a set of *roles* that can be taken by participating agents. A role can be seen as a component (or a type) that can be instantiated by agents of different types (e.g. a user can either play the role of a carpool passenger or a driver).

Each agent role (as depicted in Fig. 2, left-side) is modeled by a core process (i.e., *Agent Behavior*) and a *Scope* artifact used to understand when and how a role must be involved in a collective adaptation problem resolution. Each *Scope* is formed by an *Handler (H)* capable to catch an *Issue* and trigger the appropriate *Solver*.

Solvers model the ability of an agent to handle one or more issues. Each solver relates to the particular issue that it can handle. Moreover, each handler refers to a finite scope in the process of an agent, and it can be of two different types: (i) *external* handlers are used to catch issues coming from other agents in the system (both in the same or in a different ensembles); (ii) *internal* handlers are devoted to monitor internal property and catch the issues arising when this properties are violated.

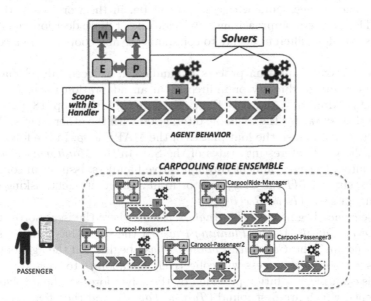

Fig. 2. Agent and ensemble models.

During the normal execution of the system, interactions between agents and ensembles are formed. Ensembles can be created spontaneously and change over time: different agents may join or leave an existing ensemble dynamically and autonomously. Their termination is also spontaneous: participants have reached their goals, or the ensemble itself has ceased to provide benefit.

For instance, in the carpooling scenario (see Fig. 2, right-side), users subscribe to a carpool ride by exploiting functionalities of the carpool manager, which has previously set up the ride and assigned a driver to it. In this way, the ensemble made by the carpool manager, the driver and the passengers is constructed[1].

During execution, the ensemble can evolve. New passengers can subscribe to the ride, while others can leave. However, to deal with unpredictable changes, local adaptation is not enough, since the scope of these changes goes beyond the single agent. Typical changes occurring in dynamic environments are characterized by the fact of affecting different agents, who can also belong to different ensembles:

- the agent directly related to the change (e.g., a ride interrupted directly affects the driver);
- the agents belonging to the same ensemble (e.g., both the passengers on board and the ones waiting at the pickup points);
- the agents involved as a consequence of the adaptation executed to solve the problem (e.g., the Carpool company provides a new plan for the waiting passengers).

This demonstrates the need for collective adaptation approaches able to deal with dynamic changes, and whose scope can be, in the worst case, the entire system. Thus, such an approach must provide one or more decision management strategies, to allow different agents to communicate and cooperate in a collective manner.

The collective adaptation process is handled in a decentralized manner by the agents involved, directly or indirectly, in an adaptation issue. Each agent implements a Monitor - Analyze - Plan - Execute (MAPE) loop [18] (as depicted in Fig. 3) that allows for the dynamic interaction with the other agents. We use a color code to distinguish the four phases of the MAPE loop. In the following, we highlight the most interesting states of the SM. In the *Monitoring phase*, each agent monitors the environment through active handlers. Issues can come either from the agent itself (*Issue Triggered*) or from a different agent, asking support for solving an issue (*Issue Received*).

The sequence begins with the *Analyze phase*, where the issue solver is called (*Local Solver Called*). In the *Planning phase*, if the solver has found a solution (*Solution Found*), the *Collective Planning phase* begins. All the agents involved in the issue resolution process will collectively collaborate to solve it.

In this example, a solution provided by the solver foresees the involvement of other agents, which are first found (*Targets Found*), and then triggered (*Issues Targeted*) to be involved in the resolution process. Once the current agent

---

[1] In this paper, we focus only on the collective adaptation aspect for agents. Their normal execution can be handled using the technique presented in [8], which is compatible with the approach we are proposing.

receives feedback from the triggered agents (*Solution Received*), it selects the best solution (*Solution Chosen*) (e.g., by applying approaches like [7,31]).

At this point, we should distinguish two cases. If the issue was triggered internally (root node edge), the agent asks the involved targets to commit their local best solution (*Ask Partners To Commit*), it waits for their commit to be done (*All Partners Commit Done*), and eventually it commits its local solution (*Commit Local Solution*). Otherwise, if the issue was coming from outside (not root node edge), the agent reports the feedback to the issues sender (*Solution Forwarded*), and it waits for a future commit (*Commit Requested*).

The agent can receive a positive or a negative reply for its proposed solution. In both cases, it executes a solution commit (*Commit Local Solution*), which will be empty in the negative case.

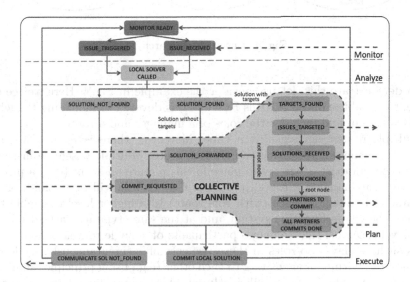

Fig. 3. MAPE state machine.

3.3 Hierarchical Adaptation

As we have seen so far, an agent instance resembles an ensemble instance in that both of them are essentially sets of role instances. However, an agent instance includes role instances belonging to different ensembles but played by a single agent. This architecture allows us to model more complex agents that can run multiple tasks simultaneously (e.g, a person can easily take/plan many activities at a time: travelling, visiting a cinema, organizing a meeting with colleagues etc.). However, a much more interesting application for agents with multiple roles is establishing links between different ensembles. If we assume that, similarly to ensemble instances, roles instances within an agent can also communicate with each other, this can be used to organize coordination of multiple ensembles.

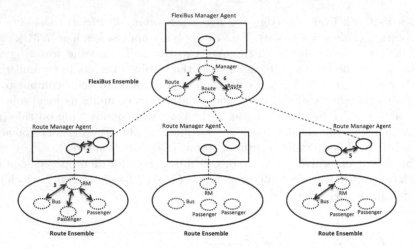

Fig. 4. Ensembles hierarchy.

To demonstrate this, let us consider the example in Fig. 4. Here we see two different ensembles: one (FlexiBus Ensemble) is devoted to managing the whole FlexiBus system and includes the roles of a manager and a route.

Multiple routes can exist at a time. Moreover, there is Route Ensemble devoted to managing a particular FlexiBus route. Multiple ensemble instances of this type can exist. If we try to place in this picture an agent (e.g., a piece of software) that manages a route, it is clear that its role will be twofold: on the one hand it is a subordinate (with role route) in a higher level ensemble that manages the whole FlexiBus system, and at the same type it is a leader in the lower level ensemble that manages participants of a single route.

As such, it plays two roles in these two ensemble simultaneously. By letting role instances within an agent talk to each other (e.g., using principles similar to issue communication), we can efficiently establish control links between ensembles. In the figure, it is exemplified with bold bidirectional arrows. For example, we can imagine that, for some intrinsic reasons, the FlexiBus manager requests a certain route to change its itinerary (e.g., in order to accommodate another passenger).

The issue communication is sent to the corresponding role instance (arrow 1). Trying to resolve this issue, the route role instance rethrows the issue to the RM role instance within the same agent (arrow 2). Consequently, the RM role instance triggers negotiation within the route ensemble to understand the possible solutions. Finally, throw the same links the resolution options are returned back to the FlexiBus manager, who makes the decision. We can see that everything works similarly to the collective adaptation within an ensemble, but now the changes happen on the inter-ensemble scale.

It is worth to remark that inter-ensemble communication can be used not only for propagating decisions to the lower level of abstraction, but also to scale up an issue in case it cannot be resolve on the lower level. For example, if the RM instance cannot resolve bus delay alone, it may scale the problem up to the level of the FlexiBus system to possibly find a solution that engages other routes (arrows 4, 5, 6). By joining all the communications into a single picture, we can derive even a more complex scenario, where the bus delay is resolved on the level of FlexiBus system (arrows 4, 5, 6) by reassigning some passengers to another route (arrows 1, 2, 3).

Even though our example shows how our architecture can be used to build arbitrarily large hierarchical systems with flexible collective adaptation, its use is not limited to hierarchies and can be exploited to design any topology based on peer-to-peer links between elements.

3.4   Collective Adaptation Engine

We have released a standalone Java implementation of the Collective Adaptation Engine (CAE), approach described in the previous sections. It has been first released as a standalone component[2], and used in the *DeMOCAS* framework [10][3].

DeMOCAS is a framework for the modeling and execution of Collective Adaptive Systems (CAS). It includes mechanisms for services specialization and adaptation using the concept of Domain Objects [9]. This allows the system to model customizable and adaptable services. DeMOCAS is build around three main aspects:

- dynamic settings: each CAS is a collection of autonomous agents entering and exiting the system dynamically;
- collaborative nature of systems: agents can collaborate in groups (i.e., ensembles) for their mutual benefit;
- collective adaptation: multiple agents must adapt their behavior in concert to respond to critical run-time impediments.

In this framework, collective adaptation is used to handle unpredictable changes, which usually affect different running agents. Collective adaptation makes the system robust and resilient in the face of situations that could cause more rigid approaches to fail. The collective adaptation is performed by exploiting the handler and solver constructs, and by associating a MAPE (Monitor, Analyze, Plan, Execute) loop to each agent, as described in previous sections.

In Fig. 5 we show the *Collective Adaptation Viewer* of DeMOCAS. This screen capture shows a report issue resolution result for an *Intense Traffic Issue* triggered by a Flexibus Driver in mid-route. On the left side, all the agents involved in the issue resolution process are listed. The issue resolution tree of the Route Manager agents that owns the solver for the triggered issue, is shown on the right side.

---

[2] For the interested reader, the prototype is available in its entirety on a GitHub repository https://github.com/das-fbk/CollectiveAdaptationEngine.

[3] https://github.com/das-fbk/DeMOCAS.

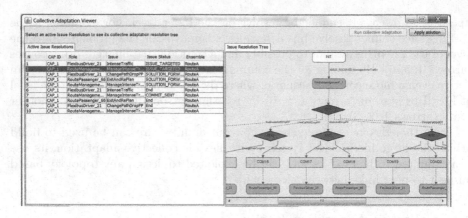

Fig. 5. Collective adaptation viewer.

This type of approach, where responsive hierarchies are loosely coupled into adaptive systems provides a war of addressing the types of system errors that can emerge when large numbers of components are tightly connected in geometrically complex networks. We discuss this in more detail in the following section.

4   Resilience Engineering for Normal Accidents

Charles Perrow established the concept of Normal Accidents [27] as property of complex, high-risk systems. These are unpredictable, yet inevitable combinations of small failures that build upon each other within an unforgiving environment. Normal accidents include catastrophic failures such as reactor meltdowns, airplane crashes, and stock market collapses. Though each failure is unique, all these failures have common properties:

- The system's components are *stiffly* connected. A change in one rapidly impacts one or more other components;
- The system is *densely* connected, so that the actions of one part affects many others, regardless of the speed of action;
- The system's internals are difficult to observe, so that failure can appear without warning.

The systems that live on the TaaS spectrum are complex - they consist of large numbers vehicles integrated in a complicated physical, electronic, and software webs. They are high risk, both at the individual level, as the vehicles themselves are inherently dangerous, and in a broader context, where misallocation of transport during an emergency could result in large scale suffering or death.

To see how easy it would be to create a single TaaS network, consider the case where blockchain-mediated transactions have become the exclusive payment scheme for transportation. There are many potential benefits for such a distributed payment system, among them a greater level of purchasing anonymity in an environment where every transaction can be tracked. But this decision to use a decentralized system means that every transaction has to have visibility to the distributed blockchain ledgers [15]. In essence, every node in the financial system is now closely coupled. If an accident occurs that breaks the network, financial transactions become impossible.

For example, consider a near-future case of a TaaS using self-driving vehicles that depends on blockchain in an island network created by an earthquake that has cut communication lines to the outside world. If the system were like the New York Stock Exchange (NYSE)[4], the entire system would suspend trading until the blockchain ledger servers could be reached, preventing evacuations. Or consider another example, where thousands of identical self-driving cars are subtly hacked so that they perceive squirrels as children in the street [24]. Adhering to the social consensus on trolley problem issues [26], thousands of self-driving cars crash into trees.

These particular accidents probably will not happen, but we can be confident that if the systems we design have Perrow's properties, something like them will. So how do we design systems for problems that are unknown? Ideally, the answer would be to ensure that any deployed systems are not densely and tightly connected, and that the elements control behavior are visible to those with the appropriate credentials.

It is not always easy to meet these three constrains short of legislation. But a proxy for addressing the stiffness and tightness of the connections in a *single* system is to ensure that *multiple, distinct* TaaS systems are always present in the communities they serve. Although each system may be dense, stiff hierarchy, the connections between the systems should be few and slack. This enforces a level of resilience at a minor cost in efficiency. Every vehicle and user doesn't need to be a individual competing across multiple markets, but neither should there only be one rigid hierarchy. We believe that *distributed ensembles is an appropriate compromise between responsiveness and resiliency.*

Acknowledgments. We'd like to thank Aaron Dant of ASRC Federal for his contribution to the direction and development of the market section of this paper.

References

1. Stock Exchange. Oxford University Press, oed online edn. http://www.oed.com. proxy-bc.researchport.umd.edu/view/Entry/190617?rskey=9zzLVE&result=2
2. Consumer spending on vehicles averaged 8427 in 2016, September 2017. https://www.bls.gov/opub/ted/2017/consumer-spending-on-vehicles-averaged-8427-in-2016.htm
3. Table 1. Median usual weekly earnings of full-time wage and salary workers by sex, quarterly averages, seasonally adjusted, October 2018. https://www.bls.gov/news.release/wkyeng.t01.htm

---

[4] https://www.nyse.com/.

4. Abeywickrama, D.B., Bicocchi, N., Zambonelli, F.: SOTA: towards a general model for self-adaptive systems. In: Reddy, S., Drira, K. (eds.) WETICE, pp. 48–53. IEEE Computer Society (2012)
5. Andres Figliozzi, M., Mahmassani, H., Jaillet, P.: Framework for study of carrier strategies in auction-based transportation marketplace. Transp. Res. Rec. J. Transp. Res. Board **1854**, 162–170 (2003)
6. Bruni, R., Corradini, A., Gadducci, F., Lluch-Lafuente, A., Vandin, A.: A conceptual framework for adaptation. In: de Lara, J., Zisman, A. (eds.) FASE 2012. LNCS, vol. 7212, pp. 240–254. Springer, Heidelberg (2012). https://doi.org/10.1007/978-3-642-28872-2_17
7. Bucchiarone, A., Dulay, N., Lavygina, A., Marconi, A., Raik, H., Russo, A.: An approach for collective adaptation in socio-technical systems. In: IEEE SASO Workshops, pp. 43–48 (2015)
8. Bucchiarone, A., Mezzina, C.A., Pistore, M., Raik, H., Valetto, G.: Collective adaptation in process-based systems. In: SASO 2014, pp. 151–156 (2014)
9. Bucchiarone, A., De Sanctis, M., Marconi, A., Pistore, M., Traverso, P.: Design for adaptation of distributed service-based systems. In: Barros, A., Grigori, D., Narendra, N.C., Dam, H.K. (eds.) ICSOC 2015. LNCS, vol. 9435, pp. 383–393. Springer, Heidelberg (2015). https://doi.org/10.1007/978-3-662-48616-0_27
10. Bucchiarone, A., De Sanctis, M., Marconi, A., Martinelli, A.: DeMOCAS: domain objects for service-based collective adaptive systems. In: Drira, K., et al. (eds.) ICSOC 2016. LNCS, vol. 10380, pp. 174–178. Springer, Cham (2017). https://doi.org/10.1007/978-3-319-68136-8_19
11. C. Pinciroli et al.: ARGoS: a modular, multi-engine simulator for heterogeneous swarm robotics. In: IROS, pp. 5027–5034 (2011)
12. Cabri, G., Puviani, M., Zambonelli, F.: Towards a taxonomy of adaptive agent-based collaboration patterns for autonomic service ensembles. In: 2011 International Conference on Collaboration Technologies and Systems, CTS 2011, Philadelphia, Pennsylvania, USA, 23–27 May 2011, pp. 508–515 (2011)
13. Clearfield, C., Tilcsik, A.: Meltdown: Why Our Systems Fail and What We Can Do About It. Atlantic Books, Penguin Canada, 20 March 2018. https://books.google.it/books/about/Meltdown.html?id=46krDwAAQBAJ&redir_esc=y
14. Crites, R.H., Barto, A.G.: Improving elevator performance using reinforcement learning. In: Advances in Neural Information Processing Systems, pp. 1017–1023 (1996)
15. Eyal, I., Sirer, E.G.: Majority is not enough: bitcoin mining is vulnerable. Commun. ACM **61**(7), 95–102 (2018)
16. Far, B.H., Wanyama, T., Soueina, S.O.: A negotiation model for large scale multi-agent systems. In: Proceedings of the 2006 IEEE International Conference on Information Reuse and Integration, IRI - 2006: Heuristic Systems Engineering, Waikoloa, Hawaii, USA, 16–18 September 2006, pp. 589–594 (2006)
17. Hölzl, M., Rauschmayer, A., Wirsing, M.: Engineering of software-intensive systems: state of the art and research challenges. In: Wirsing, M., Banâtre, J.-P., Hölzl, M., Rauschmayer, A. (eds.) Software-Intensive Systems and New Computing Paradigms. LNCS, vol. 5380, pp. 1–44. Springer, Heidelberg (2008). https://doi.org/10.1007/978-3-540-89437-7_1
18. IBM: An architectural blueprint for autonomic computing. Technical report, IBM (2006)
19. Jones, A.T., McLean, C.R.: A proposed hierarchical control model for automated manufacturing systems. J. Manuf. Syst. **5**(1), 15–25 (1986)

20. Kirilenko, A., Kyle, A.S., Samadi, M., Tuzun, T.: The flash crash: high-frequency trading in an electronic market. J. Finan. **72**(3), 967–998 (2017)
21. Levi, P., Kernbach, S.: Symbiotic-Robot Organisms: Reliability, Adaptability, Evolution, vol. 7. Springer, Heidelberg (2010). https://doi.org/10.1007/978-3-642-11692-6
22. Lima, D.: Uber caps prices ahead of Hurricane Irma's arrival, September 2017. https://www.bizjournals.com/southflorida/news/2017/09/07/ride-hailing-service-caps-prices-ahead-of.html
23. Marconi, A., Pistore, M., Traverso, P.: Automated composition of web services: the ASTRO approach. IEEE Data Eng. Bull. **31**(3), 23–26 (2008)
24. Mihajlović, M., Popovič N.: Fooling a neural network with common adversarial noise. In: 2018 19th IEEE Mediterranean Electrotechnical Conference (MELECON), pp. 293–296, May 2018. https://doi.org/10.1109/MELCON.2018.8379110
25. Nandiraju, S., Regan, A.: Freight transportation electronic marketplaces: a survey of the industry and exploration of important research issues (2008)
26. Noothigattu, R., et al.: A voting-based system for ethical decision making. CoRR abs/1709.06692 (2017). http://arxiv.org/abs/1709.06692
27. Perrow, C.: Normal Accidents: Living with High Risk Technologies-Updated Edition. Princeton University Press, Princeton (2011)
28. Popov, S.: The tangle, p. 131 (2016)
29. Quintero, R., Barbera, T.: A real-time control system methodology for developing intelligent control systems. Technical report (1992)
30. Roth, J.: The application of the hierarchy system to on-line process control. J. Br. Inst. Radio Eng. **24**(2), 117–125 (1962)
31. Saaty, T.L.: What is the analytic hierarchy process? In: Mitra, G., Greenberg, H.J., Lootsma, F.A., Rijkaert, M.J., Zimmermann, H.J. (eds.) Mathematical Models for Decision Support. NATO ASI Series, vol. 48, pp. 109–121. Springer, Heidelberg (1988). https://doi.org/10.1007/978-3-642-83555-1_5
32. Singh, M.G., Drew, S.A., Coales, J.F.: Comparisons of practical hierarchical control methods for interconnected dynamical systems. Automatica **11**(4), 331–350 (1975)
33. Tesfatsion, L.: Agent-based computational economics: modeling economies as complex adaptive systems. Inf. Sci. **149**(4), 262–268 (2003)
34. Vromant, P., Weyns, D., Malek, S., Andersson, J.: On interacting control loops in self-adaptive systems. In: IEEE/ACM SEAMS 2011, pp. 202–207 (2011)
35. Wellman, M.P.: Market-oriented programming: some early lessons. In: Clearwater, S.H. (ed.) Market-Based Control: A Paradigm for Distributed Resource Allocation, pp. 74–95. World Scientific, Singapore (1996)
36. Weyns, D., Malek, S., Andersson, J.: FORMS: unifying reference model for formal specification of distributed self-adaptive systems. TAAS **7**(1), 8 (2012)
37. Yuan, Y., Wang, F.Y.: Towards blockchain-based intelligent transportation systems. In: 2016 IEEE 19th International Conference on Intelligent Transportation Systems (ITSC), pp. 2663–2668. IEEE (2016)
38. Zambonelli, F., Bicocchi, N., Cabri, G., Leonardi, L., Puviani, M.: On self-adaptation, self-expression, and self-awareness in autonomic service component ensembles. In: SASOW, pp. 108–113 (2011)
39. Zhong, C., DeLoach, S.A.: Runtime models for automatic reorganization of multi-robot systems. In: IEEE/ACM SEAMS 2011, pp. 20–29 (2011)

CARAVAN: A Framework for Comprehensive Simulations on Massive Parallel Machines

Yohsuke Murase[1]([✉]) [iD], Hiroyasu Matsushima[2] [iD], Itsuki Noda[3] [iD],
and Tomio Kamada[1,4] [iD]

[1] RIKEN Center for Computational Science, Kobe, Hyogo 650-0047, Japan
yohsuke.murase@gmail.com
[2] School of Engineering, The University of Tokyo, Bunkyo-ku, Tokyo 113-8656, Japan
matsushima@sys.t.u-tokyo.ac.jp
[3] Artificial Intelligence Research Center, AIST, Tsukuba, Ibaraki 305-8560, Japan
i.noda@aist.go.jp
[4] Graduate School of System Informatics, Kobe University,
Kobe, Hyogo 657-8501, Japan
kamada@fine.cs.kobe-u.ac.jp

Abstract. We present a software framework called CARAVAN, which was developed for comprehensive simulations on massive parallel computers. The framework runs user-developed simulators with various input parameters in parallel without requiring the knowledge of parallel programming. The framework is useful for exploring high-dimensional parameter spaces, for which sampling points must be dynamically determined based on the previous results. Possible use cases include optimization, data assimilation, and Markov-chain Monte Carlo sampling in parameter spaces. As a demonstration, we applied CARAVAN to an evacuation planning problem in an urban area. We formulated the problem as a multi-objective optimization problem, and searched for solutions using multi-agent simulations and a multi-objective evolutionary algorithm, which were developed as modules of the framework.

Keywords: Multi-agent social simulation ·
Parameter space exploration · High-performance computing

1 Motivation and Significance

The advancement of information and communication technologies in recent decades revolutionized the study of social behavior as we gained access to the huge number of the digital records, so called "big-data", of our daily activities. Various mathematical methods and algorithms have successfully been applied to analyze these empirical data to characterize the societal activities. After empirical verification of the data, the next steps are model development and its simulations to deepen our understanding of the underlying mechanisms. Multi-agent

© Springer Nature Switzerland AG 2019
D. Lin et al. (Eds.): MMAS 2018, LNAI 11422, pp. 130–143, 2019.
https://doi.org/10.1007/978-3-030-20937-7_9

social simulation (MASS) serves as a powerful tool because social systems often demonstrate non-trivial collective phenomena that emerge from the actions of individuals, including the occurrence of traffic jams, bursty spreading of rumors on social networks, and a sudden crash in economic markets. Through the development of the models which based on the descriptions at an individual level, we are able to study the causal relationships between microscopic activities and their emergent macroscopic consequences. Moreover, well-developed MASS is expected to contribute to the better design of our social systems and services through the simulation of various possible future scenarios.

However, as discussed in [1], the application of MASS is not as straightforward as that of simulations for physical systems. One of the most critical difficulties is the fact that models for MASS are not as well established as those for physical systems. Models for MASS inevitably involve a non-negligible amount of uncertainty because individual behavior is the outcome of highly complicated intellectual, psychological, and behavioral processes that are different for each person. Furthermore, multiple social phenomena, such as the economy and traffic, may mutually interact, which makes it even more difficult to identify the factors to incorporate into a model. Even big data cannot be a solution to these problems because the data are often incomplete and biased [2] because of technical and privacy issues.

One of the methodologies to overcome these difficulties is the use of an exhaustive simulation [1]. By its nature, it is impossible to precisely predict an actual social system using a single run of MASS. Instead, it is more productive to investigate the global phase diagram of the system by running simulations with various assumptions and parameters to compensate for uncertainty. Such exhaustive simulations require both a huge amount of computational resources and effective algorithms to explore broad parameter spaces; hence, the effective application of high-performance computers (HPCs) are necessary.

In [1], Noda et al. discussed the expected computational scales for several domains of MASS and summarized them as a road map. According to the road map, although it is hypothetical, the number of required runs for a research issue in the coming decades will be order of 10^2–10^6. Although it is a so-called embarrassingly parallel problem, running such a large number of simulation jobs is not a simple issue from a technical point of view. Furthermore, intelligent algorithms for sampling parameter spaces are required as a naive random sampling would evidently be useless in a high-dimensional space. Hence, software frameworks are needed in order to correctly manage an enormous number of jobs on massive parallel computers, and to provide functions to define workflow to sample parameter spaces effectively. One of the solutions to address this problem is software called "OACIS", which manages simulation jobs automatically and provides a simple interface for users [3,4]. Although OACIS works fairly well for a wide range of problems, it can only manage up to 10^2–10^4 jobs because of the design decision to maximize usability and versatility. To manage even more jobs easily, we need another framework that is more specialized in terms of scalability.

In this article, we present a software framework called CARAVAN for parameter-space exploration on massive parallel super-computers. It was developed as an open-source software and is available on github [5]. By combining a simulator developed by a user with CARAVAN, we are able to run the simulator with various input parameters in parallel, making full use of HPCs. As shown in the next section, it scales well up to tens of thousands of processes and can manage millions of tasks. Using the framework, users become free from writing a code for parallelization using an Message Passing Interface (MPI) library because concurrent execution and scheduling of the simulation are managed by the framework. Furthermore, it is applicable not only to trivial parameter parallelization but to more complex parameter searching, such as optimization or Markov chain Monte Carlo sampling, for which sampling points are dynamically determined based on the previous results. In the next section, we illustrate the architecture of CARAVAN. Details of the implementation and its performance evaluation on the K computer are shown in Sect. 3. In Sect. 4, we present the application of CARAVAN to a MASS for evacuation guidance. In the final section, we present a summary and future perspectives.

2   Software Description

2.1   Overall Architecture

Figure 1 illustrates the architecture of CARAVAN. It consists of three modules: "search engine," "scheduler," and "simulator."

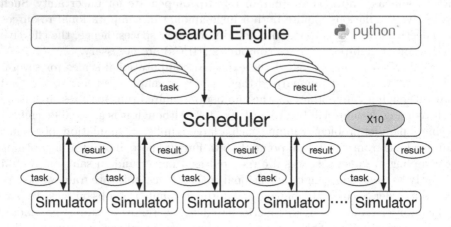

Fig. 1. An overview of the architecture of CARAVAN.

Simulator. A simulator is an executable application that the user wants to execute in parallel. It is executed as an external process by the scheduler that receives input parameters as command line arguments. A single execution of a simulator is called a "task" in CARAVAN.

Scheduler. The scheduler is the module that is responsible for parallelization. It receives commands to execute simulators from the search engine, distributes them to available nodes, and executes the simulators in parallel. This module is implemented in the X10 language [6], which is compiled into native code linked to an MPI library.

Search Engine. The search engine is a module that determines the policy on how parameter space is explored. More specifically, it generates a series of commands to be executed, that is tasks, and sends them to the scheduler. When a task is complete, the search engine receives its results from the scheduler. Based on the received results, the search engine can generate other series of tasks repeatedly. Because tasks are executed in parallel, communication between the search engine and the scheduler occurs asynchronously.

Among the three modules, users prepare a simulator and a search engine to conduct parameter-space exploration. A simulator is implemented as an executable program to be integrated into the framework. Because it is an external process, a user can implement a simulator in any language.

A search engine is the module to define the workflow of parameter-space sampling. Because parameter space is usually a high-dimensional space, various types of importance sampling, such as evolutionary optimization or Markov-chain Monte Carlo sampling, must be conducted. Hence, the parameter space to explore must be dynamically determined based on the existing simulation results, which is hard to realize with a Map-Reduce like framework. To implement such sampling algorithms, the framework provides a set of Python functions, or application programming interfaces (APIs), including ones to define callbacks which are invoked when tasks are complete.

The scheduler module is not modified by users; therefore, users do not have to write any X10 code by themselves. Once a simulator and a search engine are implemented, users can conduct parameter space exploration using tens of thousands of processors.

2.2 Requirements for a Simulator

A simulator is a stand-alone executable program that must satisfy the following requirements:

- accept parameters for simulations as command line arguments;
- generate outputs in the current directory; and
- (optional) write results to the "_results.txt" file.

First, a simulator must be prepared such that it accepts input parameters as command line arguments. This is because the scheduler receives a series of command lines from the search engine and executes them as an external process. Another requirement for a simulator is that it must generate its output files or directories in the current directory. This is because the scheduler creates a temporary directory for each task and invokes the command after setting the temporary directory as the current directory.

If a user's simulator writes a file called "_results.txt," it is parsed by the scheduler and its contents are sent back to the search engine. This is useful when a user's search engine determines the next parameters according to the simulation results. For instance, if users would like to optimize a certain value of the simulation results, they should write a value that they want to minimize (or maximize) to the "_results.txt" file. The file may contain several floating point values as its result.

2.3   Preparation of a Search Engine

The search engine is responsible for generating the command to be executed by the scheduler. An example of a minimal program for the search engine is as follows:

```
import sys
from caravan.server import Server
from caravan.task import Task

with Server.start():
    for i in range(10):
        Task.create("echo hello caravan %d" % i)
```

This sample creates a list of tasks, each of which runs the echo command. These commands are distributed to the subprocesses of the scheduler and executed in parallel.

In many applications, such as optimization, new tasks must be generated based on the results of completed tasks. Methods to define callback functions are provided for that purpose:

```
with Server.start():
    for i in range(10):
        task = Task.create("sleep %d" % (i%3+1))
        task.add_callback(lambda t, ii=i: Task.create("sleep
            %d" % (ii%3+1)))
```

If users run this program, they will find that 10 tasks are created, and 10 more tasks are created after each of the initial tasks is completed.

Although callbacks work fine, the code tends to become too complicated because of deeply nested callbacks. One of the best practices to avoid complexity is to use a "async/await" pattern, for example,

```
def run_sequential_tasks(n):
    for t in range(5):
        task = Task.create("sleep %d" % ((t+n)%3+1))
        Server.await_task(task)
        # this method blocks until the task is finished.

with Server.start():
    for n in range(3):
        Server.async( lambda n=n: run_sequential_tasks(n) )
```

This program spawns three concurrent activities, each of which executes five tasks sequentially. For each activity, a new task is created after the previous task is complete. If users visualize the results of the following program, they will see three concurrent lines of sequential tasks of length five.

In addition to the "await" method, the "await_all_tasks" method is also provided to wait for a set of tasks to complete. After awaiting tasks, users can obtain the results of the simulation runs by accessing the "results" attribute of the task. Using these methods, users can achieve a program in which tasks are created depending on the results of completed tasks.

There are also other classes and methods, such as "ParameterSet" and "Run," to simplify the implementation of Monte Carlo sampling. We do not present the full list of the APIs here. For the full documentation, please refer to the repository of CARAVAN [5].

3   Implementation

CARAVAN as a whole is executed as a single MPI job. When the MPI process starts, the rank 0 process (hereafter, the root process) invokes a Python process of the search engine as an external process. The search engine process communicates with the root process using bidirectional pipelines, thereby sending the information of simulation tasks and receiving their results. Once a series of tasks is sent to the root process, they are distributed to the other subprocesses via an MPI protocol, that is, these MPI processes work as the scheduler module. The subprocesses that receive the tasks then call the simulator, and wait until its simulation is complete. The results are parsed by the subprocesses of the scheduler, and then sent back to the search engine.

CARAVAN was designed for cases in which the duration of each task (a single run of user's simulator) typically ranges from several seconds to a few hours. CARAVAN does not perform quite well for tasks that are complete in less than a few seconds. One of the reasons for this limitation originates from the design decision that a simulator is executed as an external process. For each task, CARAVAN creates a temporary directory, creates a process, and reads a file generated by the simulator, which represents some overheads. If users would like to run fine-grained tasks, they should consider using Map-Reduce frameworks, such as [7]. Instead, the CARAVAN scheduler is designed such that it achieves ideal load balancing, even when the durations vary by orders of magnitude. Tolerance for a variation in time is essential for parameter space exploration because elapsed times typically depend significantly on the parameter values. CARAVAN was designed to scale up well to tens of thousands of MPI processes for tasks of this scale.

The scheduler module adopts the producer-consumer pattern, but with a "buffered" layer between the producer and its consumers, as shown in Fig. 2. The root process works as a producer. The producer has hundreds of buffer processes, each of which has hundreds of consumer processes. The buffered layer is introduced to prevent communication overload in a massive parallel environment. Without the buffered layer, the producer process must communicate with thousands or more consumer processes, which causes technical problems and the entire process cannot be completed normally. By introducing the buffered layer, the producer communicates only with hundreds of buffer processes. The buffer processes have their own task queues to store the tasks, and repeatedly send them to their consumers gradually, significantly reducing the amount of communication of the producer process. A similar mechanism is also adopted for the other direction of communication. The buffer processes have a store to keep the results for a short time to prevent too frequent communication. By default, CARAVAN allocates one buffer process to 384 MPI processes, which is a good parameter for a wide range of practical use cases.

The current version of CARAVAN supports only serial or multi-thread parallel programs as simulators. It cannot invoke an MPI-parallelized program as a simulator because CARAVAN launches the simulation command as an external process using a "system" command, not as an MPI process invoked by an "MPI_Comm_Spawn" function. In a future release, we plan to support MPI-parallelized simulators.

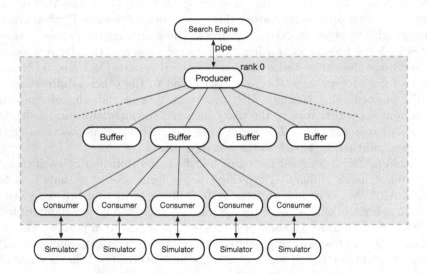

Fig. 2. The internal design of the scheduler module. Each rounded rectangle corresponds to a process. The shaded area denotes the scheduler module, which is implemented as MPI processes. The producer, which is a rank 0 MPI process, communicates with the search engine via bidirectional pipes. Tasks are distributed to buffers and then sent to their producers. Each consumer spawns a simulator process as its subprocess.

We evaluated the performance of job scheduling for the following test cases:

case 1 (TC1). At the beginning of the job, we generate N tasks. Each task takes t seconds, where t is drawn randomly from a uniform distribution $[20, 30]$.
case 2 (TC2). At the beginning of the job, we generate N tasks, whose duration t is drawn from a power law distribution of exponent -2 between $t_{min} = 5$ and $t_{max} = 100$ s.

case 3 (TC3). At the beginning of the job, we generate $N/4$ tasks. When each task is complete, another task is created until the total number of tasks reaches N. The duration of each task t is drawn randomly from a power law distribution of exponent -2 between $t_{min} = 5$ and $t_{max} = 100\,s$.

TC1 corresponds to the case in which the variation in task durations is not large. This is the easiest among the three cases because its load balancing is trivial. TC2 is more complicated because the distribution of the task durations has a heavy tail. The majority of the jobs are complete in less than $10\,s$; however, there are a certain number of tasks that run for significantly longer durations. TC3 is even more complicated because all tasks are not generated initially. Tasks are appended after the jobs are complete. We test this case because we often need to determine the parameter space to be explored depending on the results of previous tasks. For these tests, we generated dummy tasks, each of which slept for a given period of time.

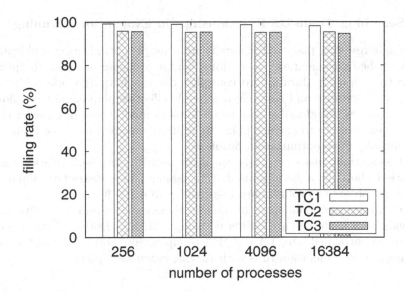

Fig. 3. Performance of the CARAVAN for the three test cases on the K computer. The job filling rates for TC1, TC2, and TC3 are depicted for several numbers of MPI processes.

We evaluated these test cases on the K computer using $N_p = 256$, 1024, 4096, and 16384 MPI processes. The number of nodes used in these tests was $N_p/8$ because a node of the K computer has eight cores and the tests were conducted as flat-MPI jobs. We used $N = 100N_p$; hence, each MPI process had 100 tasks, on average. We evaluated the performance using the job filling rate r, which we define as

$$r = \frac{\sum_i^N \left(t_i^{\text{end}} - t_i^{\text{begin}} \right)}{T * N_p}, \tag{1}$$

where t_i^{end} and t_i^{begin} are the times at which the ith task begins and ends, respectively. Total job duration T is defined as the interval between the beginning of the first task and end of the last task, that is, $T = \max\{t_i^{\text{end}}\} - \min\{t_i^{\text{begin}}\}$. The job filling rate is an indicator of the equal load balancing and the cost of inter-process communications. If the communication cost is negligible and the load is perfectly balanced, the job filling rate should reach 100%. The results of the performance evaluation on the K computer are shown in Fig. 3. As shown in the figure, the job filling rates for the three test cases were reasonably close to the optimum, which demonstrates ideal scaling up to this scale.

4   Application to Multi-agent Simulation

4.1   Searching Trade-Off Relationships in Evacuation Planning

Designing a response plan to disasters is not a simple optimization problem. For example, when designing an evacuation plan for residents, we need to optimize its effectiveness (e.g. duration to complete the evacuation) while taking into account its feasibility and cost. Even a highly effective plan cannot be adopted when it requires an infeasible cost to be implemented. There often exist trade-offs between these factors; thus, planning a disaster response can be formulated as a multi-objective optimization problem.

In this section, as a case study, we investigate the trade-off relationships of evacuation plans for a flood caused by a tsunami in a district in Japan. We use a multi-objective evolutionary algorithm (MOEA) [9] to locate the Pareto front in three-dimensional space of the effectiveness, cost, and feasibility, where these values for each plan are estimated using a MASS. (Details of the objective functions are provided later.) An MOEA is implemented on CARAVAN because it requires many simulation runs with various evacuation plans.

4.2   Multi-objective Optimization Algorithm

Multi-objective optimization involves optimizing more than one objective function simultaneously, where a number of Pareto optimal solutions exist in general. It is formulated as

$$\min\left(f_1(\mathbf{x}), f_2(\mathbf{x}), \ldots, f_k(\mathbf{x})\right), \tag{2}$$

where k is the number of objective functions and f_i is the ith objective function of a set of variables, $\mathbf{x}$. An MOEA is a variant of the evolutionary algorithm for multi-objective optimization problems, which repeats (1) parent selection, (2) crossover, (3) mutation, and (4) deletion to update the population. In this cycle, the MOEA retains good solutions in the previous generation as archived solutions. We adopt one of the most standard methods of an MOEA, the elitist non-dominated sorting genetic algorithm NSGA-II [8].

In the conventional NSGA-II, a population update is performed after the objective functions for all the individuals in the population have been calculated, that is, after multi-agent simulations that correspond to all individual cases are completed in our case. Although we can evaluate objective functions in parallel using HPCs, a naive implementation of NSGA-II may cause serious performance degradation. This is because the times required to run simulations for these individual cases may be widely different. If we wait for the completion of the calculations for all individuals, a significant amount of CPU resource is wasted because of the serious load imbalance.

To overcome this problem, we introduce an asynchronous generation-update method to NSGA-II. In our algorithm, we update a subset of the population when a certain fraction of the calculations are complete without waiting for all the simulation runs to be completed. More specifically, we prepare P_{ini} individuals at the beginning and start calculations for them. When the calculations for P_n ($< P_{ini}$) individuals are complete, they are added to the set of archived individuals. Based on the results of the archived individuals, P_n offspring are newly generated and calculations for them are started. This replacement of P_n individuals is defined as a single generation, and we repeat this process for a given number of generations. When P_n newly complete individuals are added to the archived individuals, we keep only the top $P_{archive}$ individuals selected using tournament selection on the set of archived individuals. Out of the archived individuals, P_n individuals are newly generated every generation. By introducing asynchronous updates, we can achieve a high-performance using a massive parallel computer.

In our study, $P_{ini} = 1000$, $P_n = 500$, and $P_{archive} = 1000$ were used. For each individual (i.e. input parameters of the simulator), we conducted five independent runs that had a different random number seed, and their results were averaged. Simulated binary crossover [12] and polynomial mutation [9] were used as genetic operators. For the tournament selection parameters, a crossover rate of 1.0, simulated binary crossover of $\eta_b = 15$, mutation rate of 0.01, and polynomial mutation of $\eta_p = 20$ were used.

4.3 Evacuation Simulator

To evaluate an evacuation plan, we used a multi-agent simulator Crowd-Walk [10,11], which simulates the moves of pedestrians in a city. The simulator adopts one-dimensional roads on which agents move; that is, the road network is represented by nodes and links. This design is advantageous for making simulations sufficiently fast to manage a large number of agents.

In this study, we simulated the evacuation of pedestrians in the Yodogawa district in Osaka, Japan. The road network had 2,933 nodes and 8,924 links. In our setting, the number of evacuees and shelters were 49,726 and 86, respectively. Figure 4 shows a snapshot of the simulation in this study.

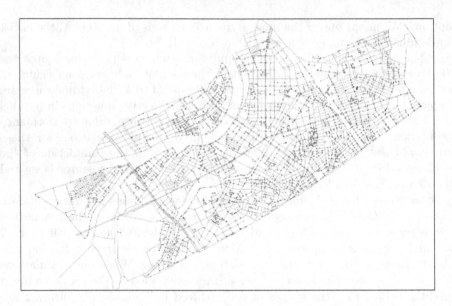

Fig. 4. Snapshot of one of the evacuation simulations conducted in this study. The lines and green points indicate roads and agents, respectively. (Color figure online)

In our study, the entire simulation area were divided into 533 sub-areas. Each sub-area had a given number of evacuees. The evacuees in each sub-area were further divided into two groups in the ratio r_i and $1 - r_i$, where i is an index of the sub-areas. For each group, a shelter was assigned as an evacuation destination. The ratios r_i and destinations for each group are input parameters that characterize an evacuation plan. Thus, we had 1,599 input parameters for this simulation as $\{r_i\}$ and two destinations were assigned to each sub-area. We fixed other simulation parameters (e.g., the speed of the pedestrians) for simplicity.

We used the following three objective functions in this study:

f1: time to complete the evacuation
Required time until all the agents arrive at their designated shelter. This is obtained from the simulation.

f2: complexity of the evacuation plan
We quantify the difficulty of the evacuation plan using the information entropy of the population distribution in each sub-area:
$f_2 = \sum_i (r_i \log(r_i) + (1 - r_i) \log(1 - r_i))$. If we do not split the residents in a sub-area into smaller groups, the evacuation plan becomes simpler. Thus, smaller entropy indicates a simpler evacuation plan. This quantity is calculated when an evacuation plan is given.

f3: number of excess evacuees
  This is a measure of the feasibility of a plan. Each shelter has a capacity, and the number of excess evacuees are measured. This quantity is calculated when an evacuation plan is given.

Solutions that minimize these objective functions were searched using NSGA-II.

4.4   Results and Discussion

We conducted an optimization on the K computer using 640 nodes and 5,120 CPU cores. The population was updated for 40 generations, and 105,000 simulation runs were conducted in total. Even though the elapsed time for each simulation run ranged significantly from 30 min to 50 min, depending on the simulation parameters, most of the simulation runs were conducted in parallel and their job balancing was good. The job filling rate achieved 93% in our experiment.

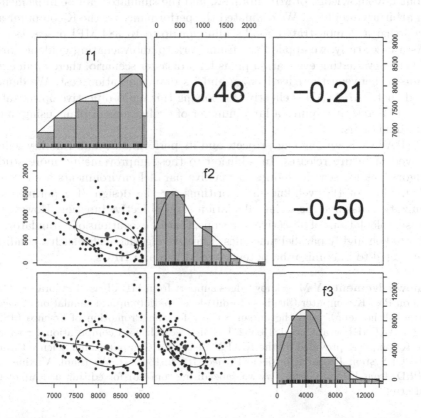

Fig. 5. Solutions obtained after 40 generations. In the left bottom panels, the solutions are shown in scatter plots, whereas their correlation coefficients are shown in the top right panels. In the diagonal panels, the histograms of the solution as a function of $f1$, $f2$, and $f3$ are shown.

Figure 5 shows the solutions determined after 40 generations. In the left bottom panels of Fig. 5, scatter plots of the solutions on the Pareto front are shown. Although they actually exist in three-dimensional space, they are mapped into two-dimensional spaces in these plots. Clearly, there are negative correlations between a pair of the objective functions. Their Pearson's correlation coefficients were calculated and are shown in the upper right panels. In the diagonal panels, the histograms of the solutions are shown. The correlation coefficients are negative, which indicates that there are trade-offs between these objective functions. For instance, if we want to shorten the time for evacuation, a complex plan is needed.

5   Conclusions and Future Work

In this paper, we presented CARAVAN, a highly scalable framework for parameter-space exploration, which executes independent simulation runs in parallel on massive parallel computers. Users can define a workflow using Python without any knowledge of MPI libraries, and the simulator can be implemented in an arbitrary language. We evaluated the performance on the K computer and showed that it demonstrated good scaling for up to 16, 384 MPI processes.

As a case study, we applied the framework to an evacuation guidance problem. When evaluating evacuation plans for a disaster scenario, there often exists a trade-off between the effectiveness and its implementation cost. We demonstrated that CARAVAN is effective for solving this multi-objective optimization problem because it requires a large number of evaluations of plans using multi-agent simulations.

CARAVAN is an ongoing project, and its performance and usability will be improved in future releases. In addition to these improvements, more studies on algorithms for search engines in massive parallel environments are strongly needed. Most of the well-known algorithms for the design of experiments or optimizations assume the serial calculation of an objective function. However, in our case, calculations of objective functions, that is, executions of a simulator, are conducted on highly parallel machines. Effective algorithms for such a condition are expected to maximize the potential of MASS and HPCs.

Acknowledgement. Y.M. acknowledges support from MEXT as "Exploratory Challenges on Post-K computer (Studies of multi-level spatiotemporal simulation of socioeconomic phenomena)" and the Japan Society for the Promotion of Science (JSPS) (JSPS KAKENHI; grant no. 18H03621). This research used computational resources of the K computer provided by the RIKEN Center for Computational Science through the HPCI System Research project (Project ID: hp160264). We thank Maxine Garcia, PhD, from Edanz Group (www.edanzediting.com/ac) for editing a draft of this manuscript.

References

1. Noda, I., et al.: Roadmap and research issues of multiagent social simulation using high-performance computing. J. Comput. Soc. Sci. **1**(1), 155–166 (2018)
2. Török, J., et al.: What big data tells: sampling the social network by communication channels. Phys. Rev. E **94**(5), 052319 (2016)
3. Murase, Y., et al.: An open-source job management framework for parameter-space exploration: OACIS. J. Phys. Conf. Ser. **921**, 012001 (2017)
4. Murase, Y., et al.: A tool for parameter-space exploration. Phys. Procedia **57**, 73–76 (2014)
5. http://github.com/crest-cassia/caravan
6. http://x10-lang.org/
7. Matsuda, M., et al.: K MapReduce: a scalable tool for data-processing and search/ensemble applications on large-scale supercomputers. In: IEEE Cluster Computing (CLUSTER) (2013)
8. Deb, K., Agrawal, S., Pratap, A., Meyarivan, T.: A fast elitist non-dominated sorting genetic algorithm for multi-objective optimization: NSGA-II. In: Schoenauer, M., Deb, K., Rudolph, G., Yao, X., Lutton, E., Merelo, J.J., Schwefel, H.-P. (eds.) PPSN 2000. LNCS, vol. 1917, pp. 849–858. Springer, Heidelberg (2000). https://doi.org/10.1007/3-540-45356-3_83
9. Deb, K.: Multiobjective Optimization using Evolutionary Algorithms. Wiley, Chichester (2001)
10. Yamashita, T., Okada, T., Noda, I.: Implementation of simulation environment for exhaustive analysis of huge-scale pedestrian flow. SICE JCMSI **6**(2), 137–146 (2013)
11. Yamashita, T., Soeda, S., Onishi, M., Noda, I.: Development and application of high-speed evacuation simulator with one-dimensional pedestrian model. J. Inform. Process. Soc. Japan **53**(7), 1732–1744 (2012)
12. Deb, K., Agrawal, R.B.: Simulated binary crossover for continuous search space. Complex Syst. **9**(2), 115–148 (1995)

BASIC: Towards a Blockchained
Agent-Based SImulator for Cities

Luana Marrocco[1], Eduardo Castelló Ferrer[2], Antonio Bucchiarone[3(✉)],
Arnaud Grignard[2], Luis Alonso[2], Kent Larson[2], and Alex 'Sandy' Pentland[2]

[1] Ecole polytechnique de Bruxelles, Université Libre de Bruxelles, Brussels, Belgium
lumarroc@ulb.ac.be
[2] MIT Media Lab, Massachusetts Institute of Technology,
Cambridge, MA 02139, USA
{ecstll,agrignar,alonsolp,kll}@media.mit.edu, pentland@mit.edu
[3] Fondazione Bruno Kessler, Via Sommarive, 18, Trento, Italy
bucchiarone@fbk.eu

Abstract. Autonomous Vehicles (AVs), drones and robots will revolutionize our way of travelling and understanding urban space. In order to operate, all of these devices are expected to collect and analyze a lot of sensitive data about our daily activities. However, current operational models for these devices have extensively relied on centralized models of managing these data. The security of these models unveiled significant issues. This paper proposes BASIC, the Blockchained Agent-based Simulator for Cities. This tool aims to verify the feasibility of the use of blockchain in simulated urban scenarios by considering the communication between agents through *smart contracts*. In order to test the proposed tool, we implemented a car-sharing model within the city of Cambridge (Massachusetts, USA). In this research, the relevant literature was explored, new methods were developed and different solutions were designed and tested. Finally, conclusions about the feasibility of the combination between blockchain technology and agent-based simulations were drawn.

Keywords: Blockchain · Smart contracts · Autonomous Vehicles ·
Data privacy · Multi-agent based simulation · Smart urban mobility

1 Introduction

In less than 50 years, the global urban population increased from 33 to 54%[1], making the economy of several countries concentrate in cities instead of being uniformly distributed. This drastically influenced the activity inside of the urban area, which highly impacts congestion, accidents and air pollution [1]. The most important source of exposure to pollution for humans is created by road vehicles

---

[1] https://data.worldbank.org/indicator/SP.URB.TOTL.IN.ZS.

© Springer Nature Switzerland AG 2019
D. Lin et al. (Eds.): MMAS 2018, LNAI 11422, pp. 144–162, 2019.
https://doi.org/10.1007/978-3-030-20937-7_10

and there already have been some attempts to estimate the impact of the pollution by changing from car to bicycle journeys [2]. Moreover, because of the high density of cities and the limited space that is available to parking, cars become an unsustainable mode of transportation [3] even if it can be more convenient in term of flexibility, celerity and comfort. In [4], it was showed that during the peak commuting hours, travel delays increased by 41%, making people more stressed in their life. Moreover, correlation was for example found between depression and traffic noise by analyzing a part of the population of Frankfurt international airport [5].

Cities are changing and urban planning became a new challenge for the world. In response to this, different tools like CityScope [6] developed by the CityScience group at MIT Media Lab were created in order to assist novel urban processes and help to visualize and understand complex urban data and interact with it by simulating modifications within the urban scenario. This type of tools help us to understand the urban impact of new technologies in our lives.

Modern cities attempt to flexibly integrate transportation options for residents and visitors to use buses, trains, taxis, bicycles and cars. They play an important role in the economy of the city and the quality of life of its residents. The inadequacy of traditional transportation models is proven by the growth of alternative and social initiatives aiming at a more flexible, customized and collective way of transport. To be collective, a mobility service should offer a way to organize teams of citizens that need to reach equal or closed destinations starting from different locations. In this context, new kinds of transportation are proposed to citizens like Mobility-on-Demand and ride-sharing transportation [7]. By using shared mobility, the notion of owning a car, using it for personal transportation and leaving it in a parking disappears and gives way to the notion of requesting and splitting a service only when it's needed. A lot of different studies aimed to quantify the impact of car sharing on car ownership and CO_2 emission [8,9], proving that this mobility actually decreases the congestion and those emissions.

In order to go even further in the congestion reduction and the mobility paradigm change, new technologies like Autonomous Vehicles (AV) were proposed because they have the potential to impact on vehicle safety, travel behavior and flow distribution [10]. These vehicles are not totally accepted yet in urban areas because some modifications in the legislation are still needed [11], but new methods are currently investigated and developed to make these vehicles more efficient in data analyzing and decision making [12]. While the National Highway Traffic Safety Administration (NHTSA) statistics tell us that human error is the main reason of road crashes, AVs allows users to enjoy their mobility by reducing the time that they have to monitor the dangers of the road [13]. In an ideal world, it seems that this technology only needs time to be accepted as a regular mode of transportation as well as bus, tram or subway. However, despite all these advantages, some barriers still remain and are the major drag for citizens and users.

Despite the fact that personalized services can be proposed to users by analyzing their personal information, the question of data privacy is becoming more and more relevant with new technologies [14]. According to the literature, 20% of the world's data was collected during this last couple of years [15] and people are starting to understand that these data actually have a real economic value [16]. Nowadays, the most common way to store and access this data is to use centralized databases [17]. However, this centralization encounters more and more issues. First, since the server is the entity that can provide the service, if it stops, the entire system will paralyze. The users will thus not be able to access to the service during the failure time. Second, there is the problem of data privacy. In most cases, all data remain unencrypted, therefore, the entity who has it in its possession can breach the privacy of users [18]. Finally, these databases can be easily modified at the server side, which means that the producers (i.e., users) of the data don't have any control over it and don't know how it is being used [19,20].

One of the most promising technologies to tackle both problems of data centralization and privacy is blockchain. More than a mean for exchanging cryptocurrencies without intermediaries, blockchain technology is starting to introduce different methods in order to achieve a secure and accountable way to share data. For instance, [21] outlined a framework for sharing machine learning models between hospitals, [22] described a method to manage byzantine agents in a swarms of robots, [23] introduced a secure architecture for Internet of things (IoT), and [24] proposed a scoring protocol for autonomous systems to increase their reputation. Complementarily, the urban mobility and smart cities fields are also paying an increasing amount of attention to this evolution. In fact, in order to achieve efficient urban mobility models and smarter cities data needs to be collected and processed to improve urban processes. This concern has driven recent works where the problem of communication among AVs was explored [25], by using a blockchain-based solution.

In response to these concerns, this work addresses the use of blockchain in the urban mobility and smart cities fields by proposing a data-sharing framework among different agents based on *smart contracts*. BASIC (Blockchained Agent-based SImulator for Cities) *aims to combine an agent-based simulator with blockchain technology in order to conduct research on urban scenarios where data are involved and needs to securely shared*. The potential of this framework is illustrated in a car-sharing service where a non-negligible number of personal data is usually collected about users with the current proposed applications. The following sections are structured as follow. Section 2 describes background notions of the simulator and the blockchain technologies used in the framework proposed. Section 3 presents the architecture of the framework and the different parts involved in it and how they interact together. Section 4 describes the results of using the proposed tool in a car-sharing scenario. Finally, Sect. 5 concludes this paper with the discussion and the future work of this simulator.

2   Background

2.1   Car-Sharing Scenario

Today, a new kind of mobility is emerging, with the aim of making our city smarter and more connected. Congestion control, autonomy of users, environmental impact and reduction of accidents are several reasons that motivate the use of Autonomous Vehicles (AVs) in urban areas. However, this new kind of mobility needs to be protected, controlled, and managed. For this purpose, we tested BASIC in a car-sharing scenario in the city of Cambridge (MA, USA), where simulated users and AVs interact. When users need to move around the city, they can request an AV, then, the system forms a group, sends the correspondent AV to users' pick-up points and finally drops them off. BASIC adds a blockchain component to achieve a secure data-sharing approach between users and AVs. BASIC should thus be able to support that kind of infrastructure and should also be stable when the number of AVs and users increase. Finally, all AVs and users have to be connected in order to avoid desynchronization issues.

2.2   Agent-Based Simulation

BASIC is based on a generic existing ABM model [26] design to be easily customized for more specific applications [27]. The ABM model is developed using Gama Platform [28][2]. GAMA allows to model and simulate spatially explicit agent-based simulations where real-world maps, streets, buildings, etc. are integrated by using GIS data. Moreover, different types of agents can be programmed each one with their own behavior and attributes. The behavior of each agent is supported by functions, which can represent reflexes (automatically called every step) or actions (executed when another part of the code calls it). To realize the motivating scenario, two agent species were coded. First, *users* were developed in order to recreate the daily activity of citizens moving from one starting location to a certain destination. Second, *AVs* were developed in order to wander around the urban area and fulfill the car-sharing application. The behavior of both species is explained with more details in Sect. 3.1.

2.3   Blockchain and *Smart Contracts*

The most famous application of blockchain is Bitcoin[3]. Bitcoin is a cryptocurrency introduced in 2008 and the idea behind it is to create a new way to make transactions between peers without a third party in a transparent and secure way. In order to send a transaction from one user to another, a peer-to-peer network is used, which allows to delete the central unit from the process.

The blockchain can be seen as a incorruptible ledger of transactions that is decentralized since the information held on it is duplicated in each one of the

---

[2] http://www.gama-platform.org/.
[3] https://bitcoin.org/.

different computers (nodes) of the peer-to-peer network. In order to add transactions in the blockchain, every nodes must verify and validate the content of the block. This technology allows thus to create *trust between agents* who don't trust in each other. Each block is composed by transactions. In each transaction, we can find the sender, the receiver, the amount but also additional information can be added. Transactions are made from one address to another. Only nodes with access to the private key of the corresponding address can make a transaction from this address (in other words, if you don't have the secret key of the address A, you will not be able to send a transaction from address A). In addition to transactions, each block contains information about previous blocks. Blocks are thus linked in a chain. Therefore, if the content of the previous block changes (for example, if someone tries to attack the system by modifying a block), the value of this information will also change and will create an inconsistency in the blockchain. For this reason, when something is written in the blockchain, it is very difficult to modify it.

A *genesis block*[4] is created as the starting point of the configuration of the chain. With this block for instance, it is possible to initialize accounts with some amount of cryptocurrency inside. This method is useful to generate tokens in the system, and can only be used when the blockchain system is in the design phase. A second way to generate tokens in the system is mining. In order to validate blocks in the blockchain, the content of the block must be first verified. This is the role of *miners*. Miners are nodes of the network. The goal of them, as we just said previously, is to verify and add blocks at the end of the blockchain. To do so, they have to compete with each other. In fact, in order to validate a block, a computational problem needs first to be solved by miners. The first miner who solves it is considered the winner and can add his block at the end of the blockchain. When a miner succeeds, he is rewarded with a certain amount of cryptocurrency (Ether[5] in case of using the Ethereum blockchain).

In our approach, the Ethereum[6] blockchain is used. The ethereum platform provides the additional capability of deploying *smart contracts*[7] in the blockchain. The advantage of *smart contracts* is that Turing-complete code can be added to the blockchain. Due to this functionality, more elaborated and autonomous operations beyond sending and receiving transactions are possible. A *smart contract* can be seen as a digital contract with rules and conditions. This code is thus composed by variables and functions and is deployed within a certain address in the blockchain. Each node of the network has the possibility to interact with the *smart contract* in a peer-to-peer way. First, interacting with the contract implies to call one of its functions. However, such operation is costly since the user needs to register a transaction in the blockchain. Second, when interacting with the *smart contract* the content of this interaction stays secret and it is held by the *smart contract*, however, the proof that this interaction took

---

[4] https://en.bitcoin.it/wiki/Genesis_block.
[5] https://www.ethereum.org/ether.
[6] https://www.ethereum.org/.
[7] https://en.wikipedia.org/wiki/Smart_contract.

```
contract AskingCar {
    struct Transaction{
        bytes32 idTransaction;
        bytes32 idPassenger;
        bytes32 idCar;
        ...
    }
    string  private idCar;
    mapping (bytes32 => Transaction) private transactions;
    bytes32[] private idsTransaction;

    /* Constructor of the contract */
    function AskingCar(string id) public {
        idCar = id;
    }

    /* Function that will add the info of the passenger */
    function addTransactionInfo(bytes32 idTrans, bytes32
        idPass, bytes32 idCar, bytes32 start, bytes32 end,
        int hour){
        var transaction = transactions[idTrans];
            transaction.idTransaction = idTrans;
            transaction.idPassenger = idPass;
            transaction.idCar = idCar;
            ...
    }

    /* Function that will add the end hour of
      the drive when the drive is finished
    */
    function addEndHour(bytes32 idTransaction, int endHour){
        if(validTransaction(idTransaction)){
            transactions[idTransaction].endHour = endHour;
        }
    }

    /*Check if the transaction is assigned to this contract*/
    function validTransaction(bytes32 idTrans) view public
        returns (bool) {
        for(uint i = 0; i < idsTransaction.length; i++) {
            if (idsTransaction[i] == idTrans) {
                return true;
            }
        }
        return false;
    }
}
```

Fig. 1. Smart contract used when a user needs an AV.

place is stored in the blockchain and remains public to its participants. Figure 1 shows a portion of a *smart contract*, implemented in each AV. It is composed by two main functions: ADDTRANSACTIONINFO, used to add info related to the user that needs an AV, and ADDENDHOUR, used to add the end hour of the journey when the user reaches her/his destination.

In this research, the ethereum network was simulated by using Docker[8]. Docker provides container-based virtualization and allows to build networks of agents running specific software in an easy way. The code used to build the containers and the simulations described in this research is publicly available in the following github repository[9].

3   The BASIC Architecture

In order to provide a modular framework that can be customized for different urban applications, BASIC's architecture has been specified and is composed by different layers, defined one above the other. A graphical representation of this stack is shown in Fig. 2. In the following sections we give a description of each layer with the aim of giving details on how the BASIC framework works.

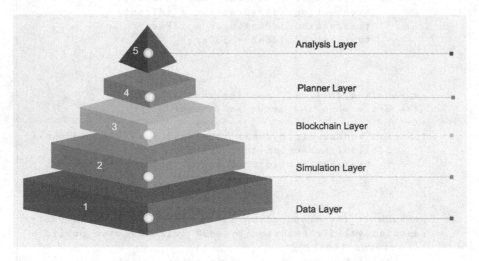

Fig. 2. Multilayer decomposition of BASIC (from bottom to top). First, the data layer represents the actual data used in order to simulate a realistic urban scenario (population information, GIS files, etc). With these data, we were able to build the second layer; the simulation layer was implemented using GAMA which provided different agents such as AVs and users. Third, the blockchain layer creates the infrastructure for the data management in the system. Four, the planner layer aims to guide the system by helping the routing and decision making processes. Finally, the analysis layer sheds some light about the feasibility of the proposed approach.

---

[8] https://www.docker.com/.
[9] https://github.com/agrignard/Basic.git.

3.1   Data and Simulation Layers

The DATA LAYER of the BASIC architecture has the objective of creating a virtual environment that replicates a realistic urban scenario.

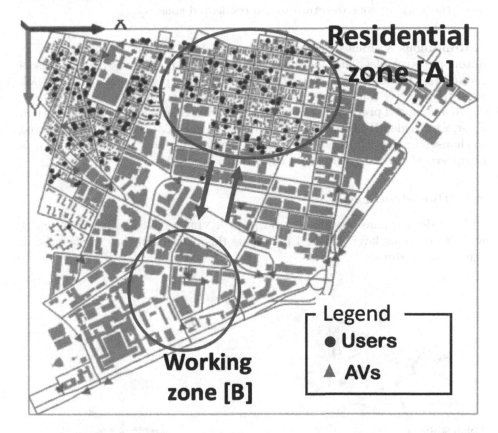

Fig. 3. Simulation of AVs (green triangles) and users (blue dots) in the Kendall urban area, in Cambridge (MA, USA). Two zones are depicted: the residential zone (A) where users live and the working zone (B) where users work. The number of users and AVs were adjusted in the image in order to increase readability. (Color figure online)

The SIMULATION LAYER is an extension of the *CityScope* framework proposed in [26] where *buildings*, *roads* and *citizens* have been already modeled and formed the starting point of our simulations. GIS files have been used in order to replicate the environment and allow us to have a representation of the Kendall area in Cambridge (MA, USA). On top of this, two types of agents have been specified:

Users. These agents represent citizens of the Kendall area. In this simulation, a simple behavior was implemented (see the User Model in Fig. 5). Each user is assigned to a residential (A) and a working (B) zone (see Fig. 3). The only possibility for the user to go between these two zones is to use an AV. All users are located in zone A when the simulation starts. Then, during the morning hours (i.e., 6–9 AM), at a random point in time, they go to work. After this, during the afternoon hours (i.e., 5–8 PM), at a random point in time, all users leave the working zone to return to the residential zone.

Autonomous Vehicles (AVs). The second class of agents of this system are autonomous vehicles. The unique role of them is to respond to the request of users around the city. Initially, they wander around the map performing a random walk until they receive a user request (see the AV Model in Fig. 6).

As mentioned previously, two types of zones are represented in the simulation. First, we can identify a residential zone (zone [A] in Fig. 3). This zone is composed by houses and apartments. In contrast, the working zone (zone [B] Fig. 3) is composed of company offices and educational institutions.

3.2   Blockchain Layer

This section explains how the BLOCKCHAIN LAYER is built and how it interacts with its previous layer. Figure 4 represents this connection that we describe in the following steps:

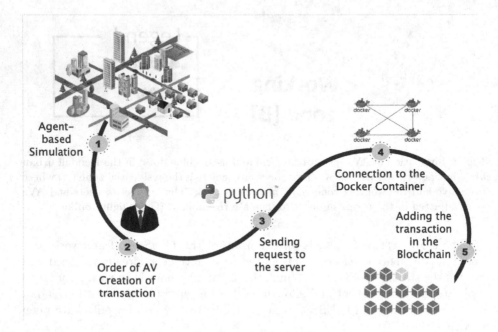

Fig. 4. Process flow of a request of a AV from a user. The starting point is the agent-based simulation. When a user needs an AVs, a transaction is created and sent to the Docker container trough a Python interface. Finally, the container will interact with the blockchain in order to add the transaction in it.

```
species User skills:[moving]{
    building home;
    building work;
    AV myAV <- nil;
    bool waitingForCar <- false;
    ...

    action movement(building start, building end){
        if(currentTransaction = nil){
            do createAndAddTransaction(start, end);
            waitTime <- step*cycle;
        }
        if(myAV = nil){
            askingForCar <- true;
            if(inAGroup = false){
                copassengers <- findPeople();
                if(length(copassengers) > 1 or (step*
                    cycle - waitTime) > maxWaitTime){
                    .....
                }
            }
        }
        if(inAGroup = true and myAV = nil){
            do findCarAndUpdateGroup;
        }
        ......
    }

    action findCarAndUpdateGroup{
        do askAV;
        loop user over: copassengers{
            user.myAV <- self.myAV;
        }
        ask myAV{
            do addPassengers(myself.copassengers);
        }
    }

    AV askAV{
        freeAVs <- AV where(each.isFree = true);
        myAV <- freeAVs closest_to(self);
        return myAV;
    }
    ....
}
```

Fig. 5. User model.

```
species AV skills:[moving, network]{
    list<point> startPoints <- [];
    list<point> endPoints <- [];
    list<User> passengers <- [];
    ...
    action dropOff(User user){
        (user.currentTransaction).endHour <- currentHour;
        ask user{
            ask userClient{
                string info <- myself.currentTransaction.
                    getStringEndHour();
                do sendMessage("User;addEndHour;","User",
                    myself.name, info);
            }
        }
        ...
    }
    action addPassengers(list<User> users){
        isFree <- false;
        self.passengers <- users;
        loop user over: users{
            add user.location to: startPoints;
              if(user.nextObjective = "home"){
              add any_point_in(user.home) to: endPoints;
            }
            else{
                add any_point_in(user.work) to: endPoints;
            }
        }
        objective <- "pickUp";
    }
}
```

Fig. 6. Autonomous Vehicle (AV) model.

1 **Agent-based simulation.** This simulation is composed by AVs and users. Each AV is associated to a mining node in the network and deploys its own *smart contract* (as shown in Fig. 1). Each user is associated to a wallet in the blockchain with a certain amount of *ether* pre-filled.

2 **Order of an AV.** When it's time to move from home to work (or vice-versa), the user needs to order a AV. Due to the interaction with the car-sharing algorithm explained in the next section, a AV is assigned to the user.

3 **Sending request to the Python server.** First, a TCP connection is made between GAMA and a Python script. Each user is connected to this code which acts as a client interface. This script acts as an interface between the simulation internals and an external system such as the blockchain. Finally, when an AV is assigned to the user (output of step 2), the same user sends

a message through this interface with the address of the *smart contract* to query (i.e., the one of the requested AV).

4 **Connection to the Docker Container.** To connect with docker, a Docker API[10] is used for the Python language. By using this API, we developed a Python client connected to Docker. Due to this connection, it is possible to enter inside the container and launch code (i.e. script for deploying or querying a contract). For the purpose of this work, we deployed a private blockchain composed of a network docker nodes. Each nodes is associated to one AV and runs geth inside.

5 **Adding the transaction in the Blockchain.** The last step of the workflow is to add the transaction in the blockchain. To this end, the web3-eth JavaScript API[11] is used. This API allows to run geth[12] commands inside of a JavaScript script, which is useful in order to interface with ethereum nodes inside the Docker container (as explained at step 4). By using the Javascript API and a network of interconnected geth nodes, the transaction can thus be sent and added to the network.

3.3   Planner Layer

As mentioned before, the PLANNER LAYER aims to coordinate the fleet of AVs in order to pick up and drop off users. For this purpose, a simple car-sharing model that aggregates users into groups is depicted in Fig. 7.

Fig. 7. Workflow of the planner layer. Step 1 consists to change the internal state of the user. By changing this variable, the system knows that this specific user needs an AV. Step 2 is the grouping phase. A car-sharing algorithm will take into account all users that need an AV in order to make groups. Finally, step 3 is route operation phase. Now that a group is formed, the assigned AV is sent to this group in order to pick users up and drop them off.

---

[10] https://docker-py.readthedocs.io/en/stable/client.html.
[11] https://web3js.readthedocs.io/en/1.0/web3-eth.html.
[12] https://github.com/ethereum/go-ethereum/wiki/geth.

This algorithm is composed of 3 main steps:

1 **Modification of the internal state of users.** In the simulation, each user has a variable which is modified when he/she needs to move. Thus, when a user needs an AV, he/she will change the value of this variable first. This change of internal state takes place at a random point in time during the morning/afternoon shifts explained in Sect. 3.1.

Algorithm 1. Formation of group for the planner layer.

1: **for** *user* in *userWithChangedState* **do**
2:     *group* ← *emptyList*
3:     add *user* in group
4:     remove *user* from *userWithChangedState*
5:     **while** user.waintingTime < maxTime AND group.length = 1 **do**
6:         **for** *other* in *userWithChangedState* **do**
7:             **if** group.length < 5 AND dist(user.start,other.start) < *ThresholdStart* AND dist(user.stop,other.stop) < *ThresholdStop* **then**
8:                 add *other* in group
9:                 remove *other* from *userWithChangedState*
10:             **end if**
11:         **end for**
12:     **end while**
13: **end for**

---

2 **Formation of a group.** The next step is the creation of groups. This process is described in Algorithm 1. In line 1, we can see that this algorithm is executed for each user with a changed state (the state is changed when a user needs an AV). A group will be assigned to this user and the idea is to add other users in this group. To do so, the block (from line 5 to 12) is executed. However, there are two conditions for the execution of this part. First, a limit of time is expressed in line 5. In fact, if a user is looking for a group but no one fits in this group, he will be able to take an AV. Second, when the group is composed of more than one user (the initial one), there is no need to execute again this loop.

Inside this block, the formation of a group is done as follows: Every other users will be taken into account (as shown in line 6), and if he meets some condition, he is added to the group. These users need to be within a threshold distance (*ThresholdStart*) from each other. Moreover, these user's destinations need to be in a place within a certain distance (*ThresholdStop*) from each other. This is represented in line 7.

3 **Route Operation.** If the conditions are met, a group is formed and the closest AV is assigned to the group. This AV picks up and drops off users by always going to the closest stop. If it is not possible to form a group, a maximum waiting time (line 5) was included to prevent lockout periods. If, after this time, the algorithm doesn't find any group, an AV is assigned to a single user as it was explained before.

4   Experiment, Results and Analysis

This section describes the last layer of the BASIC system architecture: the ANALYSIS LAYER. As described previously, during the experimental phase of this framework, the feasibility of the integration of blockchain in urban scenario was tested by implementing a car-sharing model. This model focused on the population that uses car and ride-sharing to go work. Some parameters were fixed during the experiments and are explained below:

- **Number of AVs.** In our system, the number of vehicles available in the city was fixed at ten. Because each car is a node of the blockchain network, we have thus ten mining nodes in the system. The first idea was to test the tool and its feasibility with a small amount of AVs. After doing that, extrapolations will be used to draw conclusions about the scalability of the system.
- **Period of time.** During these experiments, we analyze the behaviour of the simulation representing seven days (one week). Each day is the same and the agents have the same behaviour (i.e., go to work and go back home).
- **Distance thresholds for the grouping phase.** During the grouping phase, the distance between starting points of users was fixed to one kilometer. The exact same value was fixed for the ending points of users.
- **Maximum waiting time.** During the grouping phase, it was decided to put a limit on the time that a user can spend for finding a group. This limit was fixed at 15 min.
- **Difficulty of the blockchain.** The difficulty fixes the time needed to mine a block and therefore include new transactions. A too high difficulty value could provoke a slow-down of the system while a too low difficulty value might impact the security of the system. Therefore, in the experiments conducted in the research, we decided to fix the difficulty level.
- **Gas used.** When a transaction is made in the blockchain, it implies to pay a fee for the miner. Each user can choose the fee he/she would like to pay for the transaction by tuning the gas parameter. If the user selects a high value for the gas, the transaction will be mined faster. On the contrary, when the value of gas is low, it might take more time for the transaction to be mined. In this case, the gas was fixed at 25000000 for all transactions. This value remained fixed throughout the experiments.
- **Genesis block.** In order to initialize the blockchain, a genesis block was created. This genesis block contains accounts that were pre-filled with Ether. For the experiments described in this work, ten accounts were initially created and filled up with twenty Ether.

By using a blockchain solution for storing data, we know that a full copy of the ledger is kept in all nodes (AVs). It is important to note that, even though, recent literature suggests that storing data directly into the blockchain might impact the scalability of the system leading to bloat [29], the aim of our experiments is to analyze how much memory is needed in each AV according to the number of users in the simulation and whether a realistic projection of these requirements might exceed current state-of-the-art specifications in the AV field.

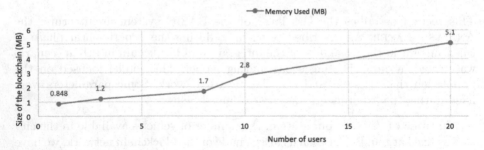

Fig. 8. Amount of memory needed for one AV (node) after seven days of operation in relation to the number of users in the simulation.

Figure 8 shows the amount of memory needed per node (AV) in relation to the number of users active in the simulation. During this test, the number of users was increased from one to twenty. This allowed us to see the evolution of the memory needed per AV. Let's remember that, each day, users need an AV to go to work in the morning, and to come back home during the afternoon. The AV is thus requested two times per day per user. The maximum number of users in an AV is fixed at five, which also correlated to the maximum capacity for user groups introduced in the previous section. According to Fig. 8, when the number of users increase, the size of the blockchain also increases. This phenomenon can be explained by the fact that the size of the blockchain is proportional to the number of transactions. If more users are present in the system, more users will need to travel and thus, more transactions will be created. Let's remember that the only way for users to move, is to use car-sharing. Everyday, each user needs two AVs. However, each request for having an AV corresponds to two transactions. The first transaction represents the request itself. Each user queries the AV by providing all the needed information like the starting and destination points, user address (public key), hour, etc. When the drive is completed, there is the second transaction. The second transaction aims to validate the drive by adding the ending hour when the user finally arrived at his destination point. In conclusion, because users need to travel two times each day, four transactions are added per user per day.

Let's now analyze the memory needed for such a system. As we can see in Fig. 9, after seven days, the size of the blockchain for this system when there is 20 users is 5.1 MB. This amount of data will be stored in each AV. By using this information, we can extrapolate what will be the size of the blockchain after a year. After 52 weeks, by making the assumption that this growth will be linear, the size will be around 265 MB. Due to previous research [6], the population in the Kendall area was roughly estimated to 10.000 people. Moreover, in 2016, 3.5% of the population in Cambridge (where Kendall belongs to) used carpooling as method of travel[13]. By using this, we can estimate the number of carpoolers to 350. By making the same linear assumption than before and by considering these 350 citizens, the amount of needed memory is thus 4641 MB (4.641 GB). Today, storing that amount of data in an AV is feasible according to current AV specifications.

5   Discussion and Future Work

During this work, we tested the feasibility of the combination between blockchain, agent-based modelling, and urban mobility by proposing a tool named BASIC. This tool was validated by implementing a car-sharing simulation within the city of Cambridge (MA, USA). The blockchain component was introduced in our work to store and share data among a distributed system of AVs and users in order to avoid a centralized controlling entity. First, this study suggests that the memory needed for each AV increased when the number of users increased. However, the simulation process was feasible and fully operational with 30 agents (20 users and 10 cars).

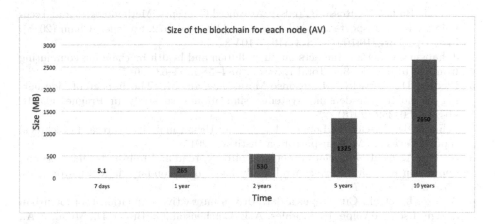

Fig. 9. Extrapolation of the memory needed for one AV (node) with 20 users.

Today, mobility in urban areas is still a big challenge and it remains complicated to test new infrastructures in real life. Due to BASIC, it is now possible to simulate different kinds of urban scenarios where agents interact with a blockchain layer. In the future, other implementation works are possible in order to increase the performance of the system. Improving the car-sharing algorithm is a first idea and will allow to have less cars in the city. The impact on the traffic will also be an interesting feature to analyze in this case. Since this research suggests that storing the data in a decentralized way is feasible, continuing with

---

[13] https://datausa.io/profile/geo/cambridge-ma/.

the idea of data privacy is an interesting direction to make citizens control their own data. Along those lines, people are realizing the real economic value of their data. Allowing them (by using the *smart contract* technology for example) to choose who can see this information, for how long, and for what purposes, can be another interesting next step that can be implemented by using BASIC. Finally, since a modern city needs to flexibly integrate transportation options including different means (i.e., cars, buses, trains, taxis, and bicycles), the combinatorial complexity of all these possibilities negates the options of a single monolithic control system. How would a grouping, or ensemble of hierarchies perform in this situation? In the near future, we want to extend our approach to deal with Collective Adaptive Systems (CAS) [30][14] able to emerge and continuous adapt in a changing environment.

Acknowledgments. This project has received funding from the European Unions Horizon 2020 research and innovation programme under the Marie Skodowska-Curie grant agreement No. 751615.

References

1. Żak, J., Hadas, Y., Rossi, R. (eds.): Advanced Concepts, Methodologies and Technologies for Transportation and Logistics. AISC, vol. 572. Springer, Cham (2018). https://doi.org/10.1007/978-3-319-57105-8
2. Johansson, C., et al.: Impacts on air pollution and health by changing commuting from car to bicycle. Sci. Total Environ. **584–585**, 55–63 (2017)
3. Fiedler, D., Certický, M., Alonso-Mora, J., Cáp, M.: The impact of ridesharing in mobility-on-demand systems: simulation case study in Prague. CoRR, abs/1807.03352 (2018)
4. Schrank, D., Eisele, B., Lomax, T., Bak, J.: Urban mobility scorecard. Technical report, Texas A&M Transportation Institute (2015)
5. Seidler, A., et al.: Association between aircraft, road and railway traffic noise and depression in a large case-control study based on secondary data. Environ. Res. **152**, 263–271 (2017)
6. Alonso, L., et al.: CityScope: a data-driven interactive simulation tool for urban design. Use case volpe. In: Morales, A.J., Gershenson, C., Braha, D., Minai, A.A., Bar-Yam, Y. (eds.) ICCS 2018. SPC, pp. 253–261. Springer, Cham (2018). https://doi.org/10.1007/978-3-319-96661-8_27
7. Chen, X., Zheng, H., Wang, Z., Chen, X.: Exploring impacts of on-demand ridesplitting on mobility via real-world ridesourcing data and questionnaires. Transportation, August 2018
8. Nijland, H., van Meerkerk, J.: Mobility and environmental impacts of car sharing in the Netherlands. Environ. Innov. Societal Transit. **23**, 84–91 (2017)
9. Giesel, F., Nobis, C.: The impact of carsharing on car ownership in German cities. Transp. Res. Procedia **19**, 215–224 (2016)
10. Fagnant, D.J., Kockelman, K.: Preparing a nation for autonomous vehicles: opportunities, barriers and policy recommendations. Transp. Res. Part A: Policy Pract. **77**, 167–181 (2015)

---

[14] http://www.focas.eu/manifesto/ - FoCAS Manifesto: A roadmap to the future of Collective Adaptive Systems.

11. BBC New: Who is responsible for a driverless car accident? BBC News Online (2015). http://www.bbc.com/news/technology-34475031
12. Millard-Ball, A.: Pedestrians, autonomous vehicles, and cities. J. Plann. Educ. Res. **38**(1), 6–12 (2018)
13. Haboucha, C.J., Ishaq, R., Shiftan, Y.: User preferences regarding autonomous vehicles. Transp. Res. Part C: Emerg. Technol. **78**, 37–49 (2017)
14. Serra, M.: An exploratory paper of the privacy paradox in the age of big data and emerging technologies. Master's thesis, KTH, School of Electrical Engineering and Computer Science (EECS) (2018)
15. Zyskind, G., Nathan, O., Pentland, A.: Decentralizing privacy: using blockchain to protect personal data. In: 2015 IEEE Symposium on Security and Privacy Workshops, SPW 2015, San Jose, CA, USA, 21–22 May 2015, pp. 180–184 (2015)
16. Oyola, J.O., Hoffman, W., Schwab, K., Marcus, A., Luzi, M.: Personal data: the emergence of a new asset class. In: An Initiative of the World Economic Forum (2011)
17. Uber's big data platform: 100+ petabytes with minute latency (2019). https://eng.uber.com/uber-big-data-platform/
18. Former employees say Lyft staffers spied on passengers (2019). https://techcrunch.com/2018/01/25/lyft-god-view/
19. Fan, L., Ramon Gil-Garcia, J., Werthmuller, D., Brian Burke, G., Hong, X.: Investigating blockchain as a data management tool for IoT devices in smart city initiatives. In: Proceedings of the 19th Annual International Conference on Digital Government Research: Governance in the Data Age, DG.O 2018, pp. 100:1–100:2. ACM, New York (2018)
20. Michelin, R.A., et al.: SpeedyChain: a framework for decoupling data from blockchain for smart cities. In: Proceedings of the 15th EAI International Conference on Mobile and Ubiquitous Systems: Computing, Networking and Services, MobiQuitous 2018, New York City, NY, USA, 5–7 November 2018, pp. 145–154 (2018)
21. Castelló Ferrer, E., Rudovic, O., Hardjono, T., Pentland, A.: RoboChain: a secure data-sharing framework for human-robot interaction. CoRR, abs/1802.04480 (2018)
22. Strobel, V., Ferrer, E.C., Dorigo, M.: Managing byzantine robots via blockchain technology in a swarm robotics collective decision making scenario. In: Proceedings of the 17th International Conference on Autonomous Agents and MultiAgent Systems, AAMAS 2018, Stockholm, Sweden, 10–15 July 2018, pp. 541–549 (2018)
23. Alphand, O., et al.: IoTChain: a blockchain security architecture for the Internet of Things. In: WCNC, pp. 1–6. IEEE (2018)
24. Alowayed, Y., Canini, M., Marcos, P., Chiesa, M., Barcellos, M.P.: Picking a partner: a fair blockchain based scoring protocol for autonomous systems. In: Proceedings of the Applied Networking Research Workshop, ANRW 2018, Montreal, QC, Canada, 16 July 2018, pp. 33–39 (2018)
25. Singh, M., Kim, S.: Branch based blockchain technology in intelligent vehicle. Comput. Netw. **145**, 219–231 (2018)
26. Grignard, A., Alonso, L., Taillandier, P., Gaudou, B., Nguyen-Huu, T., Gruel, W., Larson, K.: The impact of new mobility modes on a city: a generic approach using ABM. In: Morales, A.J., Gershenson, C., Braha, D., Minai, A.A., Bar-Yam, Y. (eds.) ICCS 2018. SPC, pp. 272–280. Springer, Cham (2018). https://doi.org/10.1007/978-3-319-96661-8_29
27. Alfeo, A.L., et al.: Urban swarms: a new approach for autonomous waste management. CoRR, abs/1810.07910 (2018)

28. Grignard, A., Taillandier, P., Gaudou, B., Vo, D.A., Huynh, N.Q., Drogoul, A.: GAMA 1.6: advancing the art of complex agent-based modeling and simulation. In: Boella, G., Elkind, E., Savarimuthu, B.T.R., Dignum, F., Purvis, M.K. (eds.) PRIMA 2013. LNCS (LNAI), vol. 8291, pp. 117–131. Springer, Heidelberg (2013). https://doi.org/10.1007/978-3-642-44927-7_9
29. Castelló Ferrer, E.: The blockchain: a new framework for robotic swarm systems. CoRR, abs/1608.00695 (2016)
30. Bucchiarone, A., De Sanctis, M., Marconi, A., Martinelli, A.: DeMOCAS: domain objects for service-based collective adaptive systems. In: Drira, K., et al. (eds.) ICSOC 2016. LNCS, vol. 10380, pp. 174–178. Springer, Cham (2017). https://doi.org/10.1007/978-3-319-68136-8_19

Author Index

Printed in the United States
By Bookmasters